H.M.S. Pinafore by Gilbert & Sullivan

or, THE LASS THAT LOVED A SAILOR

Libretto by William S. Gilbert
Music by Arthur Sullivan

The partnership between William Schwenck Gilbert and Arthur Seymour Sullivan and their canon of Savoy Operas is rightly lauded by all lovers of comic opera the world over.

Gilbert's sharp, funny words and Sullivan's deliciously lively and hummable tunes create a world that is distinctly British in view but has the world as its audience.

Both men were exceptionally talented and gifted in their own right and wrote much, often with other partners, that still stands the test of time. However, together as a team they created Light or Comic Operas of a standard that have had no rivals equal to their standard, before or since. That's quite an achievement.

To be recognised by the critics is one thing but their commercial success was incredible. The profits were astronomical, allowing for the building of their own purpose built theatre – The Savoy Theatre.

Beginning with the first of their fourteen collaborations, Thespis in 1871 and travelling through many classics including The Sorcerer (1877), H.M.S. Pinafore (1878), The Pirates of Penzance (1879), The Mikado (1885), The Gondoliers (1889) to their finale in 1896 with The Grand Duke, Gilbert & Sullivan created a legacy that is constantly revived and admired in theatres and other media to this very day.

Index of Contents

Their fourth opera and first major success: H.M.S. Pinafore; or, The Lass That Loved a Sailor debuted on May 25, 1878 at the Opera Comique and ran for 571 performances.

DRAMATIS PERSONAE
THE RT.HON SIR JOSEPH PORTER, K.C.B. (First Lord of the Admiralty).
CAPTAIN CORCORAN (Commanding H.M.S. Pinafore).
TOM TUCKER (Midshipmite).

RALPH RAKESTRAW (Able Seaman).
DICK DEADEYE (Able Seaman).
BILL BOBSTAY (Boatswain's Mate).
BOB BECKET (Carpenter's Mate).
JOSEPHINE (the Captain's Daughter).
HEBE (Sir Joseph Porter's First Cousin).
MRS. CRIPPS (LITTLE BUTTERCUP) (A Portsmouth Bumboat Woman).
First Lord's Sisters, his Cousins, his Aunts, Sailors, Marines, etc.

SCENE

ACT I—Noon. Quarter Deck of HMS Pinafore, off Portsmouth
ACT II—Night. Quarter Deck of HMS Pinafore, off Portsmouth

MUSICAL NUMBERS

Overture
ACT I
We sail the ocean blue (Sailors)
Hail! men-o'-war's men ... I'm called Little Buttercup (Buttercup)
But tell me who's the youth (Buttercup and Boatswain)
The nightingale (Ralph and Chorus of Sailors)
A maiden fair to see (Ralph and Chorus of Sailors)
My gallant crew, good morning (Captain and Chorus of Sailors)
Sir, you are sad (Buttercup and Captain)
Sorry her lot who loves too well (Josephine)
Deleted song: Reflect, my child (Captain and Josephine)
Over the bright blue sea (Chorus of Female Relatives)
Sir Joseph's barge is seen (Chorus of Sailors and Female Relatives)
Now give three cheers (Captain, Sir Joseph, Cousin Hebe and Chorus)
When I was a lad (Sir Joseph and Chorus)
For I hold that on the sea (Sir Joseph, Cousin Hebe and Chorus)
A British tar (Ralph, Boatswain, Carpenter's Mate and Chorus of Sailors)
Refrain, audacious tar (Josephine and Ralph)
Finale, Act I (Ensemble)
Can I survive this overbearing?
Oh joy, oh rapture unforeseen
Let's give three cheers for the sailor's bride
A British tar (reprise)
ACT II
(Entr'acte)
Fair moon, to thee I sing (Captain)
Things are seldom what they seem (Buttercup and Captain)
The hours creep on apace (Josephine)
Never mind the why and wherefore (Josephine, Captain and Sir Joseph)
Kind Captain, I've important information (Captain and Dick Deadeye)
Carefully on tiptoe stealing (Soli and Chorus)
Pretty daughter of mine (Captain and Ensemble) and He is an Englishman (Boatswain and Ensemble)

ACT I

SCENE—Quarter-deck of H.M.S. Pinafore. Sailors, led by BOATSWAIN, discovered cleaning brasswork, splicing rope, etc.

CHORUS
We sail the ocean blue,
And our saucy ship's a beauty;
We're sober men and true,
And attentive to our duty.
When the balls whistle free
O'er the bright blue sea,
We stand to our guns all day;
When at anchor we ride
On the Portsmouth tide,
We have plenty of time to play.

Enter LITTLE BUTTERCUP, with large basket on her arm

RECITATIVE
Hail, men-o'-war's men-safeguards of your nation
Here is an end, at last, of all privation;
You've got your play—spare all you can afford
To welcome Little Buttercup on board.

ARIA
For I'm called Little Buttercup—dear Little Buttercup,
Though I could never tell why,
But still I'm called Buttercup—poor little Buttercup,
Sweet Little Buttercup I!

I've snuff and tobaccy, and excellent jacky,
I've scissors, and watches, and knives
I've ribbons and laces to set off the faces
Of pretty young sweethearts and wives.

I've treacle and toffee, I've tea and I've coffee,
Soft tommy and succulent chops;
I've chickens and conies, and pretty polonies,
And excellent peppermint drops.

Then buy of your Buttercup—dear Little Buttercup;
Sailors should never be shy;
So, buy of your Buttercup—poor Little Buttercup;
Come, of your Buttercup buy!

BOATSWAIN
Aye, Little Buttercup—and well called—for you're the rosiest, the roundest, and the reddest beauty in all Spithead.

BUTTERCUP
Red, am I? and round—and rosy! Maybe, for I have dissembled well! But hark ye, my merry friend—hast ever thought that beneath a gay and frivolous exterior there may lurk a canker-worm which is slowly but surely eating its way into one's very heart?

BOATSWAIN
No, my lass, I can't say I've ever thought that.

Enter DICK DEADEYE. He pushes through sailors, and comes down

DICK DEADEYE
I have thought it often. (All recoil from him.)

BUTTERCUP
Yes, you look like it! What's the matter with the man? Isn't he well?

BOATSWAIN
Don't take no heed of him; that's only poor Dick Deadeye.

DICK DEADEYE
I say—it's a beast of a name, ain't it—Dick Deadeye?

BUTTERCUP
It's not a nice name.

DICK DEADEYE
I'm ugly too, ain't I?

BUTTERCUP
You are certainly plain.

DICK DEADEYE
And I'm three-cornered too, ain't I?

BUTTERCUP
You are rather triangular.

DICK DEADEYE
Ha! ha! That's it. I'm ugly, and they hate me for it; for you all hate me, don't you?

ALL
We do!

DICK DEADEYE
There!

BOATSWAIN
Well, Dick, we wouldn't go for to hurt any fellow creature's feelings, but you can't expect a chap with such a name as Dick Deadeye to be a popular character—now can you?

DICK DEADEYE
No.

BOATSWAIN
It's asking too much, ain't it?

DICK DEADEYE
It is. From such a face and form as mine the noblest sentiments sound like the black utterances of a depraved imagination It is human nature—I am resigned.

RECITATIVE

BUTTERCUP (looking down hatchway).
But, tell me—who's the youth whose faltering feet
With difficulty bear him on his course?

BOATSWAIN
That is the smartest lad in all the fleet—
Ralph Rackstraw!

BUTTERCUP
Ha! That name! Remorse! remorse!

Enter RALPH from hatchway

MADRIGAL—**RALPH**
The Nightingale
Sighed for the moon's bright ray
And told his tale
In his own melodious way!
He sang "Ah, well-a-day!"

ALL
He sang "Ah, well-a-day!"
The lowly vale
For the mountain vainly sighed,
To his humble wail

The echoing hills replied.
They sang "Ah, well-a-day!"

ALL
They sang "Ah, well-a-day!"

RECITATIVE

I know the value of a kindly chorus,
But choruses yield little consolation
When we have pain and sorrow too before us!
I love—and love, alas, above my station!

BUTTERCUP (aside)
He loves—and loves a lass above his station!

ALL (aside)
Yes, yes, the lass is much above his station!

Exit LITTLE BUTTERCUP

BALLAD —**RALPH**
A maiden fair to see,
The pearl of minstrelsy,
A bud of blushing beauty;
For whom proud nobles sigh,
And with each other vie
To do her menial's duty.

ALL
To do her menial's duty.

A suitor, lowly born,
With hopeless passion torn,
And poor beyond denying,
Has dared for her to pine
At whose exalted shrine
A world of wealth is sighing.

ALL
 A world of wealth is sighing.

Unlearned he in aught
Save that which love has taught
(For love had been his tutor);
Oh, pity, pity me—
Our captain's daughter she,
And I that lowly suitor!

ALL
And he that lowly suitor!

BOATSWAIN
Ah, my poor lad, you've climbed too high: our worthy captain's child won't have nothin' to say to a poor chap like you. Will she, lads?

ALL
No, no.

DICK DEADEYE
No, no, captains' daughters don't marry foremast hands.

ALL (recoiling from him)
Shame! shame!

BOATSWAIN
Dick Deadeye, them sentiments o' yourn are a disgrace to our common natur'.

RALPH
But it's a strange anomaly, that the daughter of a man who hails from the quarter-deck may not love another who lays out on the fore-yard arm. For a man is but a man, whether he hoists his flag at the main-truck or his slacks on the main-deck.

DICK DEADEYE
Ah, it's a queer world!

RALPH
Dick Deadeye, I have no desire to press hardly on you, but such a revolutionary sentiment is enough to make an honest sailor shudder.

BOATSWAIN
My lads, our gallant captain has come on deck; let us greet him as so brave an officer and so gallant a seaman deserves.

Enter CAPTAIN CORCORAN

RECITATIVE

CAPTAIN CORCORAN
My gallant crew, good morning.

ALL (saluting)
Sir, good morning!

CAPTAIN CORCORAN
I hope you're all quite well.

ALL (as before)
Quite well; and you, sir?

CAPTAIN CORCORAN
I am in reasonable health, and happy
To meet you all once more.

ALL (as before)
You do us proud, sir!

SONG—**CAPTAIN**

CAPTAIN CORCORAN
I am the Captain of the Pinafore;

ALL
 And a right good captain, tool
You're very, very good,
And be it understood,
I command a right good crew,

ALL
We're very, very good,
And be it understood,
He commands a right good crew.

CAPTAIN CORCORAN
Though related to a peer,
I can hand, reef, and steer,
And ship a selvagee;
I am never known to quail
At the furry of a gale,
And I'm never, never sick at sea!
ALL.
What, never?

CAPTAIN CORCORAN
No, never!

ALL
What, never?

CAPTAIN CORCORAN
Hardly ever!

ALL
He's hardly ever sick at seal

Then give three cheers, and one cheer more,
For the hardy Captain of the Pinafore!

CAPTAIN CORCORAN
I do my best to satisfy you all—

ALL
And with you we're quite content.

CAPTAIN CORCORAN
You're exceedingly polite,
And I think it only right
To return the compliment.

ALL
We're exceedingly polite,
And he thinks it's only right
To return the compliment.

CAPTAIN CORCORAN
Bad language or abuse,
I never, never use,
Whatever the emergency;
Though "Bother it" I may
Occasionally say,
I never use a big, big D—

ALL
What, never?

CAPTAIN CORCORAN
No, never!

ALL
What, never?

CAPTAIN CORCORAN
Hardly ever!

ALL
Hardly ever swears a big, big D—
Then give three cheers, and one cheer more,
For the well-bred Captain of the Pinafore!

[After song exeunt all but CAPTAIN]

Enter LITTLE BUTTERCUP

RECITATIVE

BUTTERCUP
Sir, you are sad! The silent eloquence
Of yonder tear that trembles on your eyelash
Proclaims a sorrow far more deep than common;
Confide in me—fear not—I am a mother!

CAPTAIN CORCORAN
Yes, Little Buttercup, I'm sad and sorry—
My daughter, Josephine, the fairest flower
That ever blossomed on ancestral timber,
Is sought in marriage by Sir Joseph Porter,
Our Admiralty's First Lord, but for some reason
She does not seem to tackle kindly to it.

BUTTERCUP (with emotion)
Ah, poor Sir Joseph! Ah, I know too well
The anguish of a heart that loves but vainly!
But see, here comes your most attractive daughter.
I go—Farewell!

[Exit.

CAPTAIN CORCORAN (looking after her)
A plump and pleasing person!

[Exit.

Enter JOSEPHINE, twining some flowers which she carries in a small basket

BALLAD **JOSEPHINE**
Sorry her lot who loves too well,
Heavy the heart that hopes but vainly,
Sad are the sighs that own the spell,
Uttered by eyes that speak too plainly;
Heavy the sorrow that bows the head
When love is alive and hope is dead!

Sad is the hour when sets the sun—
Dark is the night to earth's poor daughters,
When to the ark the wearied one
Flies from the empty waste of waters!
Heavy the sorrow that bows the head
When love is alive and hope is dead!

Enter CAPTAIN

CAPTAIN CORCORAN

My child, I grieve to see that you are a prey to melancholy. You should look your best to-day, for Sir Joseph Porter, K.C.B., will be here this afternoon to claim your promised hand.

JOSEPHINE

Ah, father, your words cut me to the quick. I can esteem—reverence—venerate Sir Joseph, for he is a great and good man; but oh, I cannot love him! My heart is already given.

CAPTAIN CORCORAN (aside)

It is then as I feared. (Aloud.) Given? And to whom? Not to some gilded lordling?

JOSEPHINE

No, father—the object of my love is no lordling. Oh, pity me, for he is but a humble sailor on board your own ship!

CAPTAIN CORCORAN

Impossible!

JOSEPHINE

Yes, it is true.

CAPTAIN CORCORAN

A common sailor? Oh fie!

JOSEPHINE

I blush for the weakness that allows me to cherish such a passion. I hate myself when I think of the depth to which I have stooped in permitting myself to think tenderly of one so ignobly born, but I love him! I love him! I love him! (Weeps.)

CAPTAIN CORCORAN

Come, my child, let us talk this over. In a matter of the heart I would not coerce my daughter—I attach but little value to rank or wealth, but the line must be drawn somewhere. A man in that station may be brave and worthy, but at every step he would commit solecisms that society would never pardon.

JOSEPHINE

Oh, I have thought of this night and day. But fear not, father, I have a heart, and therefore I love; but I am your daughter, and therefore I am proud. Though I carry my love with me to the tomb, he shall never, never know it.

CAPTAIN CORCORAN

You are my daughter after all. But see, Sir Joseph's barge approaches, manned by twelve trusty oarsmen and accompanied by the admiring crowd of sisters, cousins, and aunts that attend him wherever he goes. Retire, my daughter, to your cabin—take this, his photograph, with you—it may help to bring you to a more reasonable frame of mind.

JOSEPHINE

My own thoughtful father!

[Exit JOSEPHINE. CAPTAIN remains and ascends the poop-deck.

BARCAROLLE (invisible)
Over the bright blue sea
Comes Sir Joseph Porter, K.C.B.,
Wherever he may go
Bang-bang the loud nine-pounders go!
Shout o'er the bright blue sea
For Sir Joseph Porter, K.C.B.

[During this the CREW have entered on tiptoe, listening attentive to the song.

CHORUS OF SAILORS
Sir Joseph's barge is seen,
And its crowd of blushing beauties,
We hope he'll find us clean,
And attentive to our duties.
We sail, we sail the ocean blue,
And our saucy ship's a beauty.
We're sober, sober men and true
And attentive to our duty.
We're smart and sober men,
And quite devoid of fe-ar,
In all the Royal N.
None are so smart as we are.

Enter SIR JOSEPH'S FEMALE RELATIVES

(They dance round stage)

RELATIVES
Gaily tripping,
Lightly skipping,
Flock the maidens to the shipping.

SAILORS
Flags and guns and pennants dipping!
All the ladies love the shipping.

RELATIVES
Sailors sprightly
Always rightly
Welcome ladies so politely.

SAILORS
Ladies who can smile so brightly,
Sailors welcome most politely.

CAPTAIN CORCORAN (from poop)
Now give three cheers, I'll lead the way

ALL
Hurrah! hurrah! hurrah! hurray!

Enter SIR JOSEPH with COUSIN HEBE

SONG—**SIR JOSEPH**
I am the monarch of the sea,
The ruler of the Queen's Navee,
Whose praise Great Britain loudly chants.

COUSIN HEBE
And we are his sisters, and his cousins and his
aunts!

RELATIVES
And we are his sisters, and his cousins, and his aunts!

SIR JOSEPH
When at anchor here I ride,
My bosom swells with pride,
And I snap my fingers at a foeman's
taunts;

COUSIN HEBE
And so do his sisters, and his cousins, and his
aunts!

ALL
And so do his sisters, and his cousins, and his
aunts!

SIR JOSEPH
But when the breezes blow,
I generally go below,
And seek the seclusion that a cabin grants;

COUSIN HEBE
And so do his sisters, and his cousins, and his aunts!

ALL
And so do his sisters, and his cousins, and his aunts!
His sisters and his cousins,
Whom he reckons up by dozens,
And his aunts!

SONG — **SIR JOSEPH**

When I was a lad I served a term
As office boy to an Attorney's firm.
I cleaned the windows and I swept the floor,
And I polished up the handle of the big front door.
I polished up that handle so carefullee
That now I am the Ruler of the Queen's Navee!

CHORUS

He polished, etc.
As office boy I made such a mark
That they gave me the post of a junior clerk.
I served the writs with a smile so bland,
And I copied all the letters in a big round hand—
I copied all the letters in a hand so free,
That now I am the Ruler of the Queen's Navee!

CHORUS

He copied, etc.

In serving writs I made such a name
That an articled clerk I soon became;
I wore clean collars and a brand-new suit
For the pass examination at the Institute,
And that pass examination did so well for me,
That now I am the Ruler of the Queen's Navee!

CHORUS

And that pass examination, etc.

Of legal knowledge I acquired such a grip
That they took me into the partnership.
And that junior partnership, I ween,
Was the only ship that I ever had seen.
But that kind of ship so suited me,
That now I am the Ruler of the Queen's Navee!

CHORUS

But that kind, etc.

I grew so rich that I was sent
By a pocket borough into Parliament.
I always voted at my party's call,
And I never thought of thinking for myself at all.
I thought so little, they rewarded me
By making me the Ruler of the Queen's Navee!

CHORUS

He thought so little, etc.

Now landsmen all, whoever you may be,
If you want to rise to the top of the tree,
If your soul isn't fettered to an office stool,
Be careful to be guided by this golden rule—
Stick close to your desks and never go to sea,
And you all may be rulers of the Queen's Navee!

CHORUS.—Stick close, etc.

SIR JOSEPH
You've a remarkably fine crew, Captain Corcoran.

CAPTAIN CORCORAN
It is a fine crew, Sir Joseph.

SIR JOSEPH (examining a very small midshipman)
A British sailor is a splendid fellow, Captain Corcoran.

CAPTAIN CORCORAN
A splendid fellow indeed, Sir Joseph.

SIR JOSEPH
I hope you treat your crew kindly, Captain Corcoran.

CAPTAIN CORCORAN
Indeed I hope so, Sir Joseph.

SIR JOSEPH
Never forget that they are the bulwarks of England's greatness, Captain Corcoran.

CAPTAIN CORCORAN
So I have always considered them, Sir Joseph.

SIR JOSEPH. No bullying, I trust—no strong language of any kind, eh?

CAPTAIN CORCORAN
Oh, never, Sir Joseph.

SIR JOSEPH
What, never?

CAPTAIN CORCORAN
Hardly ever, Sir Joseph. They are an excellent crew, and do their work thoroughly without it.

SIR JOSEPH
Don't patronise them, sir—pray, don't patronize them.

CAPTAIN CORCORAN
Certainly not, Sir Joseph.

SIR JOSEPH
That you are their captain is an accident of birth. I cannot permit these noble fellows to be patronised because an accident of birth has placed you above them and them below you.

CAPTAIN CORCORAN
I am the last person to insult a British sailor, Sir Joseph.

SIR JOSEPH
You are the last person who did, Captain Corcoran.
Desire that splendid seaman to step forward.

(DICK comes forward)

SIR JOSEPH
No, no, the other splendid seaman.

CAPTAIN CORCORAN
Ralph Rackstraw, three paces to the front—march!

SIR JOSEPH (sternly)
If what?

CAPTAIN CORCORAN
I beg your pardon—I don't think I understand you.

SIR JOSEPH
If you please.

CAPTAIN CORCORAN
Oh, yes, of course. If you please. (RALPH steps forward.)

SIR JOSEPH
You're a remarkably fine fellow.

RALPH
Yes, your honour.

SIR JOSEPH
And a first-rate seaman, I'll be bound.

RALPH
There's not a smarter topman in the Navy, your honour, though I say it who shouldn't.

SIR JOSEPH

Not at all. Proper self-respect, nothing more. Can you dance a hornpipe?

RALPH
No, your honour.

SIR JOSEPH
That's a pity: all sailors should dance hornpipes. I will teach you one this evening, after dinner. Now tell me—don't be afraid—how does your captain treat you, eh?

RALPH
A better captain don't walk the deck, your honour.

ALL
Aye; Aye!

SIR JOSEPH
Good. I like to hear you speak well of your commanding officer; I daresay he don't deserve it, but still it does you credit. Can you sing?

RALPH
I can hum a little, your honour.

SIR JOSEPH
Then hum this at your leisure. (Giving him MS. music.) It is a song that I have composed for the use of the Royal Navy. It is designed to encourage independence of thought and action in the lower branches of the service, and to teach the principle that a British sailor is any man's equal, excepting mine. Now, Captain Corcoran, a word With you in your cabin, on a tender and sentimental subject.

CAPTAIN CORCORAN
Aye, aye,
Sir Joseph (Crossing) Boatswain, in commemoration of this joyous occasion, see that extra grog is served out to the ship's company at seven bells.

BOATSWAIN
Beg pardon. If what, your honour?

CAPTAIN CORCORAN
If what? I don't think I understand you.

BOATSWAIN
If you please, your honour.

CAPTAIN CORCORAN
What!

SIR JOSEPH
The gentleman is quite right. If you please.

CAPTAIN CORCORAN (stamping his foot impatiently)
If you please!

[Exit.

SIR JOSEPH
For I hold that on the seas
The expression, "if you please",
A particularly gentlemanly tone implants.

COUSIN HEBE
And so do his sisters, and his cousins, and his aunts!

ALL
And so do his sisters, and his cousins, and his aunts!

[Exeunt SIR JOSEPH AND RELATIVES.

BOATSWAIN
Ah! Sir Joseph's true gentleman; courteous and considerate to the very humblest.

RALPH
True, Boatswain, but we are not the very humblest. Sir Joseph has explained our true position to us. As he says, a British seaman is any man's equal excepting his, and if Sir Joseph says that, is it not our duty to believe him?

ALL
Well spoke! well spoke!

DICK DEADEYE
You're on a wrong tack, and so is he. He means well, but he don't know. When people have to obey other people's orders, equality's out of the question.

ALL (recoiling)
Horrible! horrible!

BOATSWAIN
Dick Deadeye, if you go for to infuriate this here ship's company too far, I won't answer for being able to hold 'em in. I'm shocked! that's what I am—shocked!

RALPH
Messmates, my mind's made up. I'll speak to the captain's daughter, and tell her, like an honest man, of the honest love I have for her.

ALL
Aye, aye!

RALPH

Is not my love as good as another's? Is not my heart as true as another's? Have I not hands and eyes and ears and limbs like another?

ALL
Aye, Aye!

RALPH
True, I lack birth—

BOATSWAIN
You've a berth on board this very ship.

RALPH
Well said—I had forgotten that. Messmates—what do you say? Do you approve my determination?

ALL
We do.

DICK DEADEYE
I don t.

BOATSWAIN
What is to be done with this here hopeless chap? Let us sing him the song that Sir Joseph has kindly composed for us. Perhaps it will bring this here miserable creetur to a proper state of mind.

Exit DICK

GLEE!—RALPH, BOATSWAIN, BOATSWAIN'S MATE, and CHORUS
A British tar is a soaring soul,
As free as a mountain bird,
His energetic fist should be ready to resist
A dictatorial word.
His nose should pant and his lip should curl,
His cheeks should flame and his brow should furl,
His bosom should heave and his heart should glow,
And his fist be ever ready for a knock-down blow.

CHORUS
His nose should pant, etc.

His eyes should flash with an inborn fire,
His brow with scorn be wrung;
He never should bow down to a domineering frown,
Or the tang of a tyrant tongue.
His foot should stamp and his throat should growl,
His hair should twirl and his face should scowl;
His eyes should flash and his breast protrude,
And this should be his customary attitude—(pose).

CHORUS

His foot should stamp, etc.

[All dance off excepting RALPH, who remains, leaning pensively against bulwark.

Enter JOSEPHINE from cabin

JOSEPHINE

It is useless—Sir Joseph's attentions nauseate me. I know that he is a truly great and good man, for he told me so himself, but to me he seems tedious, fretful, and dictatorial. Yet his must be a mind of no common order, or he would not dare to teach my dear father to dance a hornpipe on the cabin table. (Sees RALPH.) Ralph Rackstraw!

(Overcome by emotion.)

RALPH

Aye, lady—no other than poor Ralph Rackstraw!

JOSEPHINE (aside)

How my heart beats! (Aloud) And why poor, Ralph?

RALPH

I am poor in the essence of happiness, lady—rich only in never-ending unrest. In me there meet a combination of antithetical elements which are at eternal war with one another. Driven hither by objective influences—thither by subjective emotions—wafted one moment into blazing day, by mocking hope—plunged the next into the Cimmerian darkness of tangible despair, I am but a living ganglion of irreconcilable antagonisms. I hope I make myself clear, lady?

JOSEPHINE

Perfectly. (Aside.) His simple eloquence goes to my heart. Oh, if I dared—but no, the thought is madness! (Aloud.) Dismiss these foolish fancies, they torture you but needlessly. Come, make one effort.

RALPH (aside)

I will—one. (Aloud.) Josephine!

JOSEPHINE (Indignantly)

Sir!

RALPH

Aye, even though Jove's armoury were launched at the head of the audacious mortal whose lips, unhallowed by relationship, dared to breathe that precious word, yet would I breathe it once, and then perchance be silent evermore. Josephine, in one brief breath I will concentrate the hopes, the doubts, the anxious fears of six weary months. Josephine, I am a British sailor, and I love you!

JOSEPHINE

Sir, this audacity! (Aside.) Oh, my heart, my beating heart!
(Aloud.) This unwarrantable presumption on the part of a common sailor!

(Aside.) Common! oh, the irony of the word! (Crossing, aloud.)
Oh, sir, you forget the disparity in our ranks.

RALPH
I forget nothing, haughty lady. I love you desperately, my life is in your hand—I lay it at your feet! Give me hope, and what I lack in education and polite accomplishments, that I will endeavour to acquire. Drive me to despair, and in death alone I shall look for consolation. I am proud and cannot stoop to implore. I have spoken and I wait your word.

JOSEPHINE
You shall not wait long. Your proffered love I haughtily reject. Go, sir, and learn to cast your eyes on some village maiden in your own poor rank—they should be lowered before your captain's daughter.

DUET—JOSEPHINE and RALPH

JOSEPHINE
Refrain, audacious tar,
Your suit from pressing,
Remember what you are,
And whom addressing!
(Aside.) I'd laugh my rank to scorn
In union holy,
Were he more highly born
Or I more lowly!

RALPH.
Proud lady, have your way,
Unfeeling beauty!
You speak and I obey,
It is my duty!
I am the lowliest tar
That sails the water,
And you, proud maiden, are
My captain's daughter!
(Aside.) My heart with anguish torn
Bows down before her,
She laughs my love to scorn,
Yet I adore her!

[Repeat refrain, ensemble, then exit JOSEPHINE into cabin.

RALPH (Recit.)
Can I survive this overbearing
Or live a life of mad despairing,
My proffered love despised, rejected?
No, no, it's not to be expected!
(Calling off.)
Messmates, ahoy!

Come here! Come here!

Enter SAILORS, HEBE, and RELATIVES

ALL
Aye, aye, my boy,
What cheer, what cheer?
Now tell us, pray,
Without delay,
What does she say—
What cheer, what cheer?

RALPH (to COUSIN HEBE)
The maiden treats my suit with scorn,
Rejects my humble gift, my lady;
She says I am ignobly born,
And cuts my hopes adrift, my lady.

ALL
Oh, cruel one.

DICK DEADEYE
She spurns your suit? Oho! Oho!
I told you so, I told you so.

SAILORS and RELATIVES.
Shall we/they submit? Are we/they but slaves?
Love comes alike to high and low—
Britannia's sailors rule the waves,
And shall they stoop to insult? No!

DICK DEADEYE
You must submit, you are but slaves;
A lady she! Oho! Oho!
You lowly toilers of the waves,
She spurns you all—I told you so!

RALPH
My friends, my leave of life I'm taking,
For oh, my heart, my heart is breaking.
When I am gone, oh, prithee tell
The maid that, as I died, I loved her well!

ALL (turning away, weeping).
Of life, alas! his leave he's taking,
For ah! his faithful heart is breaking;
When he is gone we'll surely tell
The maid that, as he died, he loved her well.

[During Chorus BOATSWAIN has loaded pistol, which he hands to RALPH.

RALPH
Be warned, my messmates all
Who love in rank above you—
For Josephine I fall!

[Puts pistol to his head. All the SAILORS stop their ears.

Enter JOSEPHINE on deck

JOSEPHINE
Ah! stay your hand—I love you!

ALL
Ah! stay your hand—she loves you!

RALPH (incredulously)
Loves me?

JOSEPHINE
Loves you!

ALL
Yes, yes—ah, yes,—she loves you!

ENSEMBLE

SAILORS and RELATIVES and JOSEPHINE
Oh joy, oh rapture unforeseen,
For now the sky is all serene;
The god of day—the orb of love—
Has hung his ensign high above,
The sky is all ablaze.

With wooing words and loving song,
We'll chase the lagging hours along,
And if I find/we find the maiden coy,
I'll/We'll murmur forth decorous joy
In dreamy roundelays!

DICK DEADEYE
He thinks he's won his Josephine,
But though the sky is now serene,
A frowning thunderbolt above
May end their ill-assorted love
Which now is all ablaze.

Our captain, ere the day is gone,
Will be extremely down upon
The wicked men who art employ
To make his Josephine less coy
In many various ways.

[Exit DICK DEADEYE

JOSEPHINE
This very night,

COUSIN HEBE
With bated breath

RALPH.
And muffled oar—

JOSEPHINE
Without a light,

COUSIN HEBE
As still as death,

RALPH
We'll steal ashore

JOSEPHINE
A clergyman

RALPH
Shall make us one

BOATSWAIN
At half-past ten,

JOSEPHINE
And then we can

RALPH
Return, for none

BOATSWAIN
Can part them then!

ALL
 This very night, etc.

(DICK appears at hatchway.)

DICK DEADEYE
Forbear, nor carry out the scheme you've planned;
She is a lady—you a foremast hand!
Remember, she's your gallant captain's daughter,
And you the meanest slave that crawls the water!

ALL
Back, vermin, back,
Nor mock us!
Back, vermin, back,
You shock us!

[Exit DICK DEADEYE

Let's give three cheers for the sailor's bride
Who casts all thought of rank aside—
Who gives up home and fortune too
For the honest love of a sailor true!
For a British tar is a soaring soul
As free as a mountain bird!
His energetic fist should be ready to resist
A dictatorial word!
His foot should stamp and his throat should growl,
His hair should twirl and his face should scowl,
His eyes should flash and his breast protrude,
And this should be his customary attitude—(pose).

GENERAL DANCE

END OF ACT I

ACT II

Same Scene. Night. Awning removed. Moonlight.

CAPTAIN CORCORAN discovered singing on poop deck, and accompanying himself on a mandolin.

LITTLE BUTTERCUP seated on quarterdeck, gazing sentimentally at him.

SONG—CAPTAIN CORCORAN
Fair moon, to thee I sing,
Bright regent of the heavens,
Say, why is everything

Either at sixes or at sevens?
I have lived hitherto
Free from breath of slander,
Beloved by all my crew—
A really popular commander.
But now my kindly crew rebel,
My daughter to a tar is partial,
Sir Joseph storms, and, sad to tell,
He threatens a court martial!
Fair moon, to thee I sing,
Bright regent of the heavens,
Say, why is everything
Either at sixes or at sevens?

BUTTERCUP
How sweetly he carols forth his melody to the unconscious moon! Of whom is he thinking? Of some high-born beauty? It may be! Who is poor Little Buttercup that she should expect his glance to fall on one so lowly! And yet if he knew—if he only knew!

CAPTAIN CORCORAN (coming down)
Ah! Little Buttercup, still on board? That is not quite right, little one. It would have been more respectable to have gone on shore at dusk.

BUTTERCUP
True, dear Captain—but the recollection of your sad pale face seemed to chain me to the ship. I would fain see you smile before I go.

CAPTAIN CORCORAN
Ah! Little Buttercup, I fear it will be long before I recover my accustomed cheerfulness, for misfortunes crowd upon me, and all my old friends seem to have turned against me!

BUTTERCUP
Oh no—do not say "all", dear Captain. That were unjust to one, at least.

CAPTAIN CORCORAN
True, for you are staunch to me. (Aside.) If ever I gave my heart again, methinks it would be to such a one as this! (Aloud.) I am touched to the heart by your innocent regard for me, and were we differently situated, I think I could have returned it. But as it is, I fear I can never be more to you than a friend.

BUTTERCUP
I understand! You hold aloof from me because you are rich and lofty—and I poor and lowly. But take care! The poor bumboat woman has gipsy blood in her veins, and she can read destinies.

CAPTAIN CORCORAN
Destinies?

BUTTERCUP
There is a change in store for you!

CAPTAIN CORCORAN
A change?

BUTTERCUP
Aye—be prepared!

DUET—LITTLE BUTTERCUP and CAPTAIN

BUTTERCUP
Things are seldom what they seem,
Skim milk masquerades as cream;
Highlows pass as patent leathers;
Jackdaws strut in peacock's feathers.

CAPTAIN CORCORAN (puzzled)
Very true,
So they do.

BUTTERCUP
Black sheep dwell in every fold;
All that glitters is not gold;
Storks turn out to be but logs;
Bulls are but inflated frogs.

CAPTAIN CORCORAN (puzzled)
So they be,
Frequentlee.

BUTTERCUP
Drops the wind and stops the mill;
Turbot is ambitious brill;
Gild the farthing if you will,
Yet it is a farthing still.

CAPTAIN CORCORAN (puzzled)
Yes, I know.
That is so.
Though to catch your drift I'm striving,
It is shady—it is shady;
I don't see at what you're driving,
Mystic lady—mystic lady.
(Aside.)   Stern conviction's o'er me stealing,
That the mystic lady's dealing
In oracular revealing.

BUTTERCUP (aside)
Stern conviction's o'er him stealing,

That the mystic lady's dealing
In oracular revealing.
Yes, I know—
That is so!

CAPTAIN CORCORAN
Though I'm anything but clever,
I could talk like that for ever:
Once a cat was killed by care;
Only brave deserve the fair.
Very true,
So they do.

CAPTAIN CORCORAN
Wink is often good as nod;
Spoils the child who spares the rod;
Thirsty lambs run foxy dangers;
Dogs are found in many mangers.

BUTTERCUP
Frequentlee,
I agree.
Paw of cat the chestnut snatches;
Worn-out garments show new patches;
Only count the chick that hatches;
Men are grown-up catchy-catchies.

BUTTERCUP
Yes, I know,
That is so.
(Aside.)   Though to catch my drift he's striving,
I'll dissemble—I'll dissemble;
When he sees at what I'm driving,
Let him tremble—let him tremble!

ENSEMBLE
Though a mystic tone I/You borrow,
You will/I shall learn the truth with sorrow,
Here to-day and gone to-morrow;
Yes, I know—
That is so!

[At the end exit LITTLE BUTTERCUP melodramatically.

CAPTAIN CORCORAN
Incomprehensible as her utterances are, I nevertheless feel that they are dictated by a sincere regard for me. But to what new misery is she referring? Time alone can tell!

Enter SIR JOSEPH

SIR JOSEPH
Captain Corcoran, I am much disappointed with your daughter. In fact, I don't think she will do.

CAPTAIN CORCORAN
She won't do, Sir Joseph!

SIR JOSEPH
I'm afraid not. The fact is, that although I have urged my suit with as much eloquence as is consistent with an official utterance, I have done so hitherto without success. How do you account for this?

CAPTAIN CORCORAN
Really, Sir Joseph, I hardly know. Josephine is of course sensible of your condescension.

SIR JOSEPH
She naturally would be.

CAPTAIN CORCORAN
But perhaps your exalted rank dazzles her.

SIR JOSEPH
You think it does?

CAPTAIN CORCORAN
I can hardly say; but she is a modest girl, and her social position is far below your own. It may be that she feels she is not worthy of you.

SIR JOSEPH
That is really a very sensible suggestion, and displays more knowledge of human nature than I had given you credit for.

CAPTAIN CORCORAN
See, she comes. If your lordship would kindly reason with her and assure her officially that it is a standing rule at the Admiralty that love levels all ranks, her respect for an official utterance might induce her to look upon your offer in its proper light.

SIR JOSEPH
It is not unlikely. I will adopt your suggestion.
But soft, she is here. Let us withdraw, and watch our opportunity.

Enter JOSEPHINE from cabin. FIRST LORD and CAPTAIN retire

SCENE—**JOSEPHINE**
The hours creep on apace,
My guilty heart is quaking!
Oh, that I might retrace
The step that I am taking!

Its folly it were easy to be showing,
What I am giving up and whither going.
On the one hand, papa's luxurious home,
Hung with ancestral armour and old brasses,
Carved oak and tapestry from distant Rome,
Rare "blue and white" Venetian finger-glasses,
Rich oriental rugs, luxurious sofa pillows,
And everything that isn't old, from Gillow's.
And on the other, a dark and dingy room,
In some back street with stuffy children crying,
Where organs yell, and clacking housewives fume,
And clothes are hanging out all day a-drying.
With one cracked looking-glass to see your face in,
And dinner served up in a pudding basin!

A simple sailor, lowly born,
Unlettered and unknown,
Who toils for bread from early morn
Till half the night has flown!
No golden rank can he impart—
No wealth of house or land—
No fortune save his trusty heart
And honest brown right hand!
And yet he is so wondrous fair
That love for one so passing rare,
So peerless in his manly beauty,
Were little else than solemn duty!
Oh, god of love, and god of reason, say,
Which of you twain shall my poor heart obey!

SIR JOSEPH and CAPTAIN enter

SIR JOSEPH
Madam, it has been represented to me that you are appalled by my exalted rank. I desire to convey to you officially my assurance, that if your hesitation is attributable to that circumstance, it is uncalled for.

JOSEPHINE
Oh! then your lordship is of opinion that married happiness is not inconsistent with discrepancy in rank?

SIR JOSEPH
I am officially of that opinion.

JOSEPHINE
That the high and the lowly may be truly happy together, provided that they truly love one another?

SIR JOSEPH
Madam, I desire to convey to you officially my opinion that love is a platform upon which all ranks meet.

JOSEPHINE

I thank you, Sir Joseph. I did hesitate, but I will hesitate no longer. (Aside.) He little thinks how eloquently he has pleaded his rival's cause!

TRIO

FIRST LORD, CAPTAIN, and JOSEPHINE

CAPTAIN CORCORAN

Never mind the why and wherefore,
Love can level ranks, and therefore,
Though his lordship's station's mighty,
Though stupendous be his brain,
Though your tastes are mean and flighty
And your fortune poor and plain,

CAPTAIN CORCORAN and **SIR JOSEPH**

Ring the merry bells on board-ship,

SIR JOSEPH

Rend the air with warbling wild,
For the union of his/my lordship
With a humble captain's child!

CAPTAIN CORCORAN

For a humble captain's daughter—

JOSEPHINE

For a gallant captain's daughter—

SIR JOSEPH

And a lord who rules the water—

JOSEPHINE (aside)

And a tar who ploughs the water!

ALL

Let the air with joy be laden,
Rend with songs the air above,
For the union of a maiden
With the man who owns her love!

SIR JOSEPH

Never mind the why and wherefore,
Love can level ranks, and therefore,
Though your nautical relation (alluding to CAPTAIN CORCORAN)
In my set could scarcely pass—
Though you occupy a station

In the lower middle class—

CAPTAIN CORCORAN and SIR JOSEPH
Ring the merry bells on board-ship,
Rend the air with warbling wild,
For the union of my/your lordship
With a humble captain's child!

CAPTAIN CORCORAN
For a humble captain's daughter—

JOSEPHINE
For a gallant captain's daughter—

SIR JOSEPH
And a lord who rules the water—

JOSEPHINE (aside)
And a tar who ploughs the water!

ALL
Let the air with joy be laden,
Rend with songs the air above,
For the union of a maiden
With the man who owns her love!

JOSEPHINE
Never mind the why and wherefore,
Love can level ranks, and therefore
I admit the jurisdiction;
Ably have you played your part;
You have carried firm conviction
To my hesitating heart.

CAPTAIN CORCORAN and SIR JOSEPH
Ring the merry bells on board-ship,
Rend the air with warbling wild,
For the union of my/his lordship
With a humble captain's child!

CAPTAIN CORCORAN
For a humble captain's daughter—

JOSEPHINE
For a gallant captain's daughter—

SIR JOSEPH
And a lord who rules the water—

JOSEPHINE (aside).
And a tar who ploughs the water!
(Aloud.) Let the air with joy be laden.

CAPTAIN CORCORAN and SIR JOSEPH
Ring the merry bells on board-ship—

JOSEPHINE
For the union of a maiden—

CAPTAIN CORCORAN and SIR JOSEPH
For her union with his lordship.

ALL
Rend with songs the air above
For the man who owns her love!

[Exit JOSEPHINE

CAPTAIN CORCORAN
Sir Joseph, I cannot express to you my delight at the happy result of your eloquence. Your argument was unanswerable.

SIR JOSEPH
Captain Corcoran, it is one of the happiest characteristics of this glorious country that official utterances are invariably regarded as unanswerable.

[Exit SIR JOSEPH.

CAPTAIN CORCORAN
At last my fond hopes are to be crowned. My only daughter is to be the bride of a Cabinet Minister. The prospect is Elysian.

(During this speech DICK DEADEYE has entered.)

DICK DEADEYE
Captain.

CAPTAIN CORCORAN
Deadeye! You here? Don't! (Recoiling from him.)

DICK DEADEYE
Ah, don't shrink from me, Captain. I'm unpleasant to look at, and my name's agin me, but I ain't as bad as I seem.

CAPTAIN CORCORAN
What would you with me?

DICK (mysteriously)
I'm come to give you warning.

CAPTAIN CORCORAN
Indeed! do you propose to leave the Navy then?

DICK DEADEYE
No, no, you misunderstand me; listen!

DUET

CAPTAIN and DICK DEADEYE

DICK DEADEYE
Kind Captain, I've important information,
Sing hey, the kind commander that you are,
About a certain intimate relation,
Sing hey, the merry maiden and the tar.

BOTH
The merry maiden and the tar.

CAPTAIN CORCORAN
Good fellow, in conundrums you are speaking,
Sing hey, the mystic sailor that you are;
The answer to them vainly I am seeking;
Sing hey, the merry maiden and the tar.

BOTH
The merry maiden and the tar.

DICK DEADEYE
Kind Captain, your young lady is a-sighing,
Sing hey, the simple captain that you are,
This very might with Rackstraw to be flying;
Sing hey, the merry maiden and the tar.

BOTH
The merry maiden and the tar.

CAPTAIN CORCORAN
Good fellow, you have given timely warning,
Sing hey, the thoughtful sailor that you are,
I'll talk to Master Rackstraw in the morning:
Sing hey, the cat-o'-nine-tails and the tar.

(Producing a "cat".)

BOTH
The merry cat-o'-nine-tails and the tar!

CAPTAIN CORCORAN
Dick Deadeye—I thank you for your warning—I will at once take means to arrest their flight. This boat cloak will afford me ample disguise—So! (Envelops himself in a mysterious cloak, holding it before his face.)

DICK DEADEYE
Ha, ha! They are foiled—foiled—foiled!

Enter CREW on tiptoe, with RALPH and BOATSWAIN meeting JOSEPHINE, who enters from cabin on tiptoe, with bundle of necessaries, and accompanied by LITTLE BUTTERCUP.

ENSEMBLE
Carefully on tiptoe stealing,
Breathing gently as we may,
Every step with caution feeling,
We will softly steal away.

(CAPTAIN stamps)—Chord.

ALL (much alarmed)
Goodness me—
Why, what was that?

DICK DEADEYE
Silent be,
It was the cat!

ALL (reassured).
It was—it was the cat!

CAPTAIN CORCORAN (producing cat-o'-nine-tails)
They're right, it was the cat!

ALL
Pull ashore, in fashion steady,
Hymen will defray the fare,
For a clergyman is ready
To unite the happy pair!

(Stamp as before, and Chord.)

ALL
Goodness me,
Why, what was that?

DICK DEADEYE
Silent be,
Again the cat!

ALL
It was again that cat!

CAPTAIN CORCORAN (aside).
They're right, it was the cat!

CAPTAIN CORCORAN (throwing off cloak).
Hold! (ALL start.)
Pretty daughter of mine,
I insist upon knowing
Where you may be going
With these sons of the brine,
For my excellent crew,
Though foes they could thump any,
Are scarcely fit company,
My daughter, for you.

CREW
Now, hark at that, do!
Though foes we could thump any,
We are scarcely fit company
For a lady like you!

RALPH
Proud officer, that haughty lip uncurl!
Vain man, suppress that supercilious sneer,
For I have dared to love your matchless girl,
A fact well known to all my messmates here!

CAPTAIN CORCORAN
Oh, horror!

RALPH and **JOSEPHINE**
I/He humble, poor, and lowly born,
The meanest in the port division—
The butt of epauletted scorn—
The mark of quarter-deck derision—
Have/Has dare to raise my/his wormy eyes
Above the dust to which you'd mould me/him
In manhood's glorious pride to rise,
I am/he is an Englishman—behold me/him

ALL

He is an Englishman!

BOATSWAIN
He is an Englishman!
For he himself has said it,
And it's greatly to his credit,
That he is an Englishman!

ALL
That he is an Englishman!

BOATSWAIN
For he might have been a Roosian,
A French, or Turk, or Proosian,
Or perhaps Itali-an!

ALL
Or perhaps Itali-an!

BOATSWAIN
But in spite of all temptations
To belong to other nations,
He remains an Englishman!

ALL
For in spite of all temptations, etc.

CAPTAIN CORCORAN (trying to repress his anger).
In uttering a reprobation
To any British tar,
I try to speak with moderation,
But you have gone too far.
I'm very sorry to disparage
A humble foremast lad,
But to seek your captain's child in marriage,
Why damme, it's too bad

[During this, COUSIN HEBE and FEMALE RELATIVES have entered.]

ALL (shocked).
Oh!

CAPTAIN CORCORAN
Yes, damme, it's too bad!

ALL
Oh!

CAPTAIN CORCORAN and DICK DEADEYE
Yes, damme, it s too bad.

[During this, SIR JOSEPH has appeared on poop-deck. He is horrified at the bad language.

COUSIN HEBE
Did you hear him? Did you hear him?
Oh, the monster overbearing!
Don't go near him—don't go near him—
He is swearing—he is swearing!

SIR JOSEPH
My pain and my distress,
I find it is not easy to express;
My amazement—my surprise—
You may learn from the expression of my eyes!

CAPTAIN CORCORAN
My lord—one word—the facts are not before you
The word was injudicious, I allow—
But hear my explanation, I implore you,
And you will be indignant too, I vow!

SIR JOSEPH.
I will hear of no defence,
Attempt none if you're sensible.
That word of evil sense
Is wholly indefensible.
Go, ribald, get you hence
To your cabin with celerity.
This is the consequence
Of ill-advised asperity

[Exit CAPTAIN, disgraced, followed by JOSEPHINE

ALL
This is the consequence,
Of ill-advised asperity!

SIR JOSEPH
For I'll teach you all, ere long,
To refrain from language strong
For I haven't any sympathy for ill-bred
taunts!

COUSIN HEBE
No more have his sisters, nor his cousins,
nor his

aunts.

ALL
For he is an Englishman, etc.

SIR JOSEPH
Now, tell me, my fine fellow—for you are a fine fellow—

RALPH
Yes, your honour.

SIR JOSEPH
How came your captain so far to forget himself? I am quite sure you had given him no cause for annoyance.

RALPH
Please your honour, it was thus-wise. You see I'm only a topman-a mere foremast hand—

SIR JOSEPH
Don't be ashamed of that. Your position as a topman is a very exalted one.

RALPH
Well, your honour, love burns as brightly in the fo'c'sle as it does on the quarter-deck, and Josephine is the fairest bud that ever blossomed upon the tree of a poor fellow's wildest hopes.

Enter JOSEPHINE; she rushes to RALPH'S arms

JOSEPHINE
Darling! (SIR JOSEPH horrified.)

RALPH
She is the figurehead of my ship of life—the bright beacon that guides me into my port of happiness—that the rarest, the purest gem that ever sparkled on a poor but worthy fellow's trusting brow!

ALL
Very pretty, very pretty!

SIR JOSEPH
Insolent sailor, you shall repent this outrage.
Seize him!

(Two MARINES seize him and handcuff him.)

JOSEPHINE
Oh, Sir Joseph, spare him, for I love him tenderly.

SIR JOSEPH

Pray, don't. I will teach this presumptuous mariner to discipline his affections. Have you such a thing as a dungeon on board?

ALL
We have!

DICK DEADEYE
They have!

SIR JOSEPH
Then load him with chains and take him there at once!

OCTETTE

RALPH
Farewell, my own,
Light of my life, farewell!
For crime unknown
I go to a dungeon cell.

JOSEPHINE
I will atone.
In the meantime farewell!
And all alone
Rejoice in your dungeon cell!

SIR JOSEPH
A bone, a bone
I'll pick with this sailor fell;
Let him be shown at once
At once to his dungeon cell.

BOATSWAIN, DICK DEADEYE, and COUSIN HEBE
He'll hear no tone
Of the maiden he loves so well!
No telephone
Communicates with his cell!

BUTTERCUP (mysteriously)
But when is known
The secret I have to tell,
Wide will be thrown
The door of his dungeon cell.

ALL
For crime unknown
He goes to a dungeon cell!

[RALPH is led off in custody.

SIR JOSEPH.
My pain and my distress
Again it is not easy to express.
My amazement, my surprise,
Again you may discover from my eyes.

ALL
How terrible the aspect of his eyes!

BUTTERCUP
Hold! Ere upon your loss
You lay much stress,
A long-concealed crime
I would confess.

SONG—**BUTTERCUP**
A many years ago,
When I was young and charming,
As some of you may know,
I practised baby-farming.

ALL
Now this is most alarming!
When she was young and charming,
She practised baby-farming,
A many years ago.

BUTTERCUP
Two tender babes I nursed:
One was of low condition,
The other, upper crust,
A regular patrician.

ALL (explaining to each other).
Now, this is the position:
One was of low condition,
The other a patrician,
A many years ago.

BUTTERCUP
Oh, bitter is my cup!
However could I do it?
I mixed those children up,
And not a creature knew it!

ALL

However could you do it?
Some day, no doubt, you'll rue it,
Although no creature knew it,
So many years ago.

BUTTERCUP
In time each little waif
Forsook his foster-mother,
The well born babe was Ralph—
Your captain was the other!!!

ALL
They left their foster-mother,
The one was Ralph, our brother,
Our captain was the other,
A many years ago.

SIR JOSEPH
Then I am to understand that Captain Corcoran and Ralph were exchanged in childhood's happy hour—that Ralph is really the Captain, and the Captain is Ralph?

BUTTERCUP
That is the idea I intended to convey, officially!

SIR JOSEPH
And very well you have conveyed it.

BUTTERCUP
Aye! aye! yer 'onour.

SIR JOSEPH
Dear me! Let them appear before me, at once!

[RALPH. enters as CAPTAIN; CAPTAIN as a common sailor. JOSEPHINE rushes to his arms

JOSEPHINE
My father—a common sailor!

CAPTAIN CORCORAN
It is hard, is it not, my dear?

SIR JOSEPH
This is a very singular occurrence; I congratulate you both. (To RALPH.) Desire that remarkably fine seaman to step forward.

RALPH
Corcoran
Three paces to the front—march!

CAPTAIN CORCORAN
If what?

RALPH
If what? I don't think I understand you.

CAPTAIN CORCORAN
If you please.

SIR JOSEPH
The gentleman is quite right. If you please.

RALPH
Oh! If you please.

(CAPTAIN steps forward.)

SIR JOSEPH (to CAPTAIN).
You are an extremely fine fellow.

CAPTAIN CORCORAN
Yes, your honour.

SIR JOSEPH
So it seems that you were Ralph, and Ralph was you.

CAPTAIN CORCORAN
So it seems, your honour.

SIR JOSEPH
Well, I need not tell you that after this change in your condition, a marriage with your daughter will be out of the question.

CAPTAIN CORCORAN
Don't say that, your honour—love levels all ranks.

SIR JOSEPH
It does to a considerable extent, but it does not level them as much as that. (Handing JOSEPHINE to RALPH.) Here — take her, sir, and mind you treat her kindly.

RALPH and JOSEPHINE
Oh bliss, oh rapture!

CAPTAIN CORCORAN and BUTTERCUP
Oh rapture, oh bliss!

SIR JOSEPH.

Sad my lot and sorry,
What shall I do? I cannot live alone!

COUSIN HEBE
Fear nothing—while I live I'll not desert you.
I'll soothe and comfort your declining days.

SIR JOSEPH
No, don't do that.

COUSIN HEBE
Yes, but indeed I'd rather—

SIR JOSEPH (resigned).
To-morrow morn our vows shall all be plighted,
Three loving pairs on the same day united!

QUARTETTE

JOSEPHINE, HEBE, RALPH, and DEADEYE
Oh joy, oh rapture unforeseen,
The clouded sky is now serene,
The god of day—the orb of love,
Has hung his ensign high above,
The sky is all ablaze.

With wooing words and loving song,
We'll chase the lagging hours along,
And if he finds/I find the maiden coy,
We'll murmur forth decorous joy,
In dreamy roundelay.

CAPTAIN CORCORAN
For he's the Captain of the Pinafore.

ALL
And a right good captain too!

CAPTAIN CORCORAN
And though before my fall
I was captain of you all,
I'm a member of the crew.

ALL
 Although before his fall, etc.

CAPTAIN CORCORAN
I shall marry with a wife,

In my humble rank of life! (turning to BUTTERCUP)
And you, my own, are she—
I must wander to and fro;
But wherever I may go,
I shall never be untrue to thee!

ALL
What, never?

CAPTAIN CORCORAN
No, never!

ALL
What, never!

CAPTAIN CORCORAN
Hardly ever!

ALL
Hardly ever be untrue to thee.
Then give three cheers, and one cheer more
For the former Captain of the Pinafore.

BUTTERCUP
For he loves Little Buttercup, dear Little
Buttercup,
Though I could never tell why;
But still he loves Buttercup, poor Little
Buttercup,
Sweet Little Buttercup, aye!

ALL
For he loves, etc.

SIR JOSEPH
I'm the monarch of the sea,
And when I've married thee (to COUSIN HEBE),
I'll be true to the devotion that my love implants,

COUSIN HEBE
Then good-bye to his sisters, and his cousins, and his aunts,
Especially his cousins,
Whom he reckons up by dozens,
His sisters, and his cousins, and his aunts!

ALL
For he is an Englishman,
And he himself hath said it,

And it's greatly to his credit
That he is an Englishman!

CURTAIN

W.S. Gilbert – A Short Biography

Sir William Schwenck Gilbert was born on November 18th, 1836 at 17 Southampton Street, Strand, London. His father, also named William, was a naval surgeon, who later became a writer of novels and short stories, some of which were illustrated by his son. Gilbert's mother was the former Anne Mary Bye Morris (1812–1888), the daughter of Thomas Morris, an apothecary.

Gilbert's parents were distant and stern, and there was no close bond between either themselves or their children (the marriage was to eventually break up in 1876). Gilbert had three younger sisters, Jane Morris, Anne Maude Mary Florence.

As a child, Gilbert was nicknamed "Bab".

The family travelled to Italy in 1838 and then France before finally returning to settle in London in 1847.

Gilbert was educated in Boulogne, France from age seven, then at Western Grammar School, Brompton, London, before the Great Ealing School, where he became head boy and wrote plays for school performances. He then attended King's College London, graduating in 1856.

His first thought for a career was to take examinations for a commission in the Royal Artillery, but the Crimean War had just ended and with fewer recruits needed only a commission in a line regiment was available. He opted instead for the Civil Service and was an assistant clerk in the Privy Council Office for four years. He hated it. In 1859 he joined the Militia, a part-time volunteer force, and served until 1878, as his other work allowed, and reached the rank of Captain.

To supplement his income Gilbert wrote a variety of stories, comic rants, theatre reviews (many in the form of a parody of the play being reviewed), and, using the pseudonym of his childhood nickname, "Bab" illustrated poems for several comic magazines, primarily Fun, started in 1861. His work was also published in the Cornhill Magazine, London Society, Tinsley's Magazine and Temple Bar. Gilbert was also the London correspondent for L'Invalide Russe and a drama critic for the Illustrated London Times. In the 1860s he also contributed to Tom Hood's Christmas annuals, to Saturday Night, the Comic News and the Savage Club Papers.

The poems, illustrated humorously by Gilbert, proved immensely popular and were reprinted in book form as the Bab Ballads. He would later return to many of these as source material for his plays and comic operas.

In 1863 he received a bequest of £300 allowing him to leave the civil service and attempt a career as a barrister. Unfortunately, he managed to attract few clients.

However, these events happily coincided with his first professionally produced play; Uncle Baby, which ran for seven weeks in the autumn of 1863.

In 1865–66, Gilbert collaborated with Charles Millward on several pantomimes, including Hush-a-Bye, Baby, On the Tree Top, or, Harlequin Fortunia, King Frog of Frog Island, and the Magic Toys of Lowther Arcade (1866).

Gilbert's first solo success, however, came a few days after Hush-a-Bye Baby premiered. His friend and mentor, Tom Robertson, was asked to deliver a pantomime within two weeks. Robertson couldn't and recommended Gilbert who took the job. Written and rushed to the stage in 10 days, Dulcamara, or the Little Duck and the Great Quack, a burlesque of Gaetano Donizetti's L'elisir d'amore, proved very popular. This led to a long series of further Gilbert opera burlesques, pantomimes and farces, full of dreadful puns, but showing signs of the satire that would later be such an integral part of Gilbert's work.

After a failed relationship with the novelist Annie Thomas, Gilbert married Lucy Agnes Turner, whom he affectionately called "Kitty", in 1867; she was 11 years his junior. They were socially active both in London and later at their new home at Grim's Dyke, often holding dinner parties. Although they had no children they had many pets, including several exotic ones.

Next followed Gilbert's biggest success so far; his penultimate operatic parody, Robert the Devil, a burlesque of Giacomo Meyerbeer's opera, Robert le diable, part of a triple bill that opened the Gaiety Theatre, London in 1868. It ran for over 100 nights.

In Victorian theatre, Gilbert's burlesques were considered very tasteful compared to the offerings of others. He would now move away from burlesque to plays with original plots and fewer puns. His first was An Old Score in 1869.

Theatre, at this time had fallen into disrepute. London was awash with poorly translated French operettas and cheaply written, prurient Victorian burlesques. From 1869 to 1875, Gilbert joined with Thomas German Reed (and his wife Priscilla), whose Gallery of Illustration sought to regain some of theatre's lost respect with family entertainments. This would be so successful that by 1885 Gilbert could safely state that original British plays were appropriate for an innocent 15-year-old girl to watch.

The initial work for the Gallery of Illustration, No Cards, was the first of six musical entertainments for the German Reeds, by Gilbert some with music composed by Thomas German Reed.

The German Reeds' intimate theatre allowed Gilbert to develop a personal style that would also cede to him control all aspects of production; set, costumes, direction and stage management.

Gilbert's first big hit at the Gallery of Illustration, Ages Ago, also opened in 1869. It marked the beginning of a collaboration with the composer Frederic Clay that would last seven years and cover four works. It was at a rehearsal for Ages Ago that Clay introduced Gilbert to Arthur Sullivan.

These musical works gave Gilbert a valuable education as a lyricist and he perfected the 'topsy-turvy' style that he had been developing in his Bab Ballads, where the humour was derived by setting up a ridiculous premise and following through on its logical consequences, however absurd they might be.

Ever busy he found time to create several 'fairy comedies' at the Haymarket Theatre. The premise was the idea of self-revelation by characters under the influence of magic or some supernatural experience. The first was The Palace of Truth (1870), based partly on a story by Madame de Genlis. In 1871, with Pygmalion and Galatea, one of seven plays that he produced that year, Gilbert scored his greatest hit to date. Together, these plays including The Wicked World (1873), Sweethearts (1874), and Broken Hearts (1875), did for Gilbert on the dramatic stage what the German Reed entertainments had done for him on the musical stage: they established that his talents were large and burgeoning, a writer of wide range, as comfortable with human drama as much as farcical humour.

Contemptorous with this period Gilbert pushed the satirical boundaries. He collaborated with Gilbert Arthur à Beckett on The Happy Land (1873), in part, a parody of his own The Wicked World, which was briefly banned because of its caricatures of Gladstone and his ministers. Similarly, The Realm of Joy (1873) was set in the lobby of a theatre performing a scandalous play (implied to be the Happy Land), with many jokes at the expense of the Lord Chamberlain (the "Lord High Disinfectant", as he's referred to in the play). In Charity (1874), however, Gilbert uses the freedom of the stage in a different way: to illuminate the contrasting ways in which society treated men and women who had sex outside of marriage. It was ground breaking and some see it as anticipating the 'problem plays' of Shaw and Ibsen.

Once established as a writer Gilbert was also the stage director, with strong, forceful opinions on how they should best be performed.

In Gilbert's 1874 burlesque, Rosencrantz and Guildenstern, the character Hamlet, in his speech to the players, sums up Gilbert's theory of comic acting: "I hold that there is no such antick fellow as your bombastical hero who doth so earnestly spout forth his folly as to make his hearers believe that he is unconscious of all incongruity". Again some say with this he prepared the ground for playwrights such as George Bernard Shaw and Oscar Wilde to be able to flourish.

Tom Robertson had "introduced Gilbert both to the revolutionary notion of disciplined rehearsals and to mise-en-scène or unity of style in the whole presentation – direction, design, music, acting." Like Robertson, Gilbert demanded discipline in his actors, that they know their lines, enunciate them clearly and keep to his stage directions, a new development for actors at the time. It also ushered in the replacement of the star with the disciplined ensemble.

Gilbert was meticulous in his preparations, making models of the stage and designing every action in advance. He refused to work with actors who challenged him. He was famous for demonstrating the action himself, even as he grew older. Such was his interest in standards that even during long runs and revivals, he closely supervised the performances of his plays, making sure that no one made additions or deletions.

Arthur Sullivan – A Short Biography

Sir Arthur Seymour Sullivan, MVO was born on May 13th 1842 in Lambeth, London. His father, Thomas Sullivan, a military bandmaster, clarinetist and music teacher, was born in Ireland and raised in Chelsea, London, and his mother, Mary Clementina (née Coghlan, English born, of Irish and Italian descent. Thomas Sullivan was based from 1845 to 1857 at the Royal Military College, Sandhurst, where he was the bandmaster and taught music privately to supplement his income. Young Sullivan became proficient with many of the instruments in the band and had composed an anthem, "By the waters of Babylon", by the age of eight. While proudly observing his son's obvious musical talent, he knew, at first hand, how insecure a profession it was and discouraged him from pursuing it.

Three years later whilst at a private school in Bayswater, Sullivan persuaded his parents and headmaster to allow him to apply for membership in the choir of the Chapel Royal. There were concerns that Sullivan at nearly 12 years of age was too old to be a treble as his voice would soon break. But he was accepted and soon became a soloist and, by 1856, was promoted to "first boy". Troublingly, even at this age, Sullivan's health was delicate, and he was easily fatigued.

However, Sullivan flourished under the training of the Reverend Thomas Helmore, and began to compose anthems and songs. Helmore arranged for one pieces, "O Israel", to be published in 1855.

In 1856, the Royal Academy of Music awarded the first Mendelssohn Scholarship to the 14-year-old Sullivan, granting him a year's training at the academy. His principal teacher there was John Goss, whose own teacher had been a pupil of Mozart. Initially Sullivan studied piano.

Sullivan's scholarship was extended to a second year, and then a third so that he could study in Germany, at the Leipzig Conservatoire. There he was trained in Mendelssohn's ideas and techniques as well as being exposed to Schubert, Verdi, Bach, and Wagner. Sullivan was an eager pupil and always looking for inspiration. On a visit to a synagogue, he was so struck by some of the cadences and progressions in the music that three decades later he would recall them for use in his serious opera, Ivanhoe.

Though the scholarship in Leipzig, was for one year he stayed for three. Sullivan credited his Leipzig period with rapid and sustained musical growth. His graduation piece, in 1861, was a set of incidental music to Shakespeare's The Tempest. Revised and expanded, it was performed at the Crystal Palace in 1862, a year after his return to London. It was an immediate sensation. He began building a reputation as England's most promising young composer.

He now embarked on composing with a series of ambitious works, interspersed with hymns, parlour songs and other light pieces of a more commercial nature. These compositions could not support him financially, and from 1861 to 1872 he supplemented his income working as a church organist, a task he enjoyed, and as a music teacher, sometimes at the Crystal Palace School, which he hated and gave up as soon as his finances allowed. Sullivan also took an early chance to compose pieces for royalty with the wedding of the Prince of Wales in 1863.

Sullivan began to put voice and orchestra together with The Masque at Kenilworth (Birmingham Festival, 1864). For Covent Garden that same year he composed his first ballet, L'Île Enchantée.

1865 saw Sullivan initiated into Freemasonry and was Grand Organist of the United Grand Lodge of England in 1887 during Queen Victoria's Golden Jubilee.

In 1866, he premiered his Irish Symphony and Cello Concerto, his only works in these genres. In the same year, his Overture in C (In Memoriam), commemorating the recent death of his father, was a commission from the Norwich Festival.

His overture Marmion was premiered by the Philharmonic Society in 1867. The Times called it "another step in advance on the part of the only composer of any remarkable promise that just at present we can boast."

Sadly, his initial attempt at opera, The Sapphire Necklace (1863–64) with a libretto by Henry F. Chorley, was not produced and, apart from the Overture and two songs published separately, is now lost.

His first surviving opera, Cox and Box (1866), was written for a private performance. It then received charity performances in London and Manchester, and was later produced at the Gallery of Illustration, where it ran for an extraordinary 264 performances. His soon to be partner, W. S. Gilbert, writing in Fun magazine, announced the score as superior to F. C. Burnand's libretto.

In 1867 Sullivan and Burnand were commissioned by Thomas German Reed for a two-act opera, The Contrabandista (revised and expanded as The Chieftain in 1894), but it was a much more modest success.

Sullivan wrote a group of seven part songs in 1868, the best-known of which is "The Long Day Closes". His last major work of the 1860s was a short oratorio, The Prodigal Son, which premiered in Worcester Cathedral as part of the 1869 Three Choirs Festival to much praise.

The Overture di Ballo, Sullivan's most enduring work, was composed for the Birmingham Festival in 1870.

1871 was a busy year. Sullivan published his only song cycle, The Window; or, The Songs of the Wrens, to words by Tennyson, and wrote the first of a series of suites of incidental music for West End productions of Shakespeare plays. Later in the year he composed a dramatic cantata, On Shore and Sea, for the opening of the London International Exhibition, and the beautiful hymn Onward, Christian Soldiers, with words by Sabine Baring-Gould. The Salvation Army adopted it and it has become one of Britain's best loved hymns.

Gilbert & Sullivan – The Collaboration Begins

In 1871, John Hollingshead commissioned Gilbert to work with Sullivan on a holiday piece for Christmas, entitled Thespis, or The Gods Grown Old, at the Gaiety Theatre. It was a success and its run was extended beyond the length of the Gaiety's normal run. And that seemed to be that.

Gilbert and Sullivan now went their separate ways. Gilbert worked again with Clay on Happy Arcadia (1872), and with Alfred Cellier on Topsyturveydom (1874), as well as several farces, operetta libretti, extravaganzas, fairy comedies, adaptations from novels, translations from the French. In 1874, he published his last piece for Fun magazine ("Rosencrantz and Guildenstern"), almost three years after his last and then promptly resigned citing disapproval of the new owner's other publishing interests.

Sullivan was busy on large-scale works in the early 1870s with the Festival Te Deum (Crystal Palace, 1872); and the oratorio, The Light of the World (Birmingham Festival, 1873). He also wrote suites of incidental music for productions of The Merry Wives of Windsor at the Gaiety in 1874 and Henry VIII at the Theatre Royal, Manchester in 1877 as well as continuing composing hymns.

In 1873, Sullivan had also contributed songs to Burnand's Christmas "drawing room extravaganza", The Miller and His Man.

By 1875 conditions were right for Gilbert and Sullivan to work together again. Back in 1868, Gilbert had published a short comedic libretto in Fun magazine entitled "Trial by Jury: An Operetta". In 1873, Gilbert had arranged with theatrical manager and composer, Carl Rosa, to expand this work into a one-act libretto. It was arranged that Rosa's wife was to sing the role of the plaintiff. Tragically, Rosa's wife died in childbirth in 1874. Gilbert offered the libretto to Richard D'Oyly Carte, but Carte could not use the piece at that time.

The project seemed grounded. A few months later Carte, was managing the Royalty Theatre, needed a short piece to pair with Offenbach's La Périchole. Carte had previously conducted Sullivan's Cox and Box and remembering that Gilbert had suggested a libretto to him, he reunited Gilbert and Sullivan. The result was the one-act comic opera Trial by Jury. Starring Sullivan's brother Fred as the Learned Judge, it became a surprise hit, as well as earning lavish praise from the critics. It played for over 300 performances in its first few seasons.

A short time after Trial had opened Sullivan wrote The Zoo, another one-act comic opera, with a libretto by B. C. Stephenson. It did not perform well. Now the path was clear for Gilbert & Sullivan to reteam together in earnest and dominate light opera for the next 15 years.

Light opera was not considered of much worth by serious critics. Gilbert wanted greater respect for himself and his profession. At that time plays were not published in a form suitable for a "gentleman's library", they were in the main cheap and unattractive in their look designed mainly for use by actors rather than the home reader. Gilbert now arranged in late 1875 for the publishers Chatto and Windus to print a volume of his plays in a format designed to appeal to the general reader, with an attractive binding and clear type, containing Gilbert's most respectable plays, including his most serious works, and mischievously capped off with Trial by Jury.

After the success of Trial by Jury, there were discussions towards reviving Thespis, but Gilbert and Sullivan were not able to agree on terms with Carte and his backers. The score to Thespis was never published, and tragically most of the music is now lost.

Carte took some time to gather together funds for another opera, and in this gap the ever-busy Gilbert produced several works including Tom Cobb (1875), Eyes and No Eyes (1875), and Princess Toto (1876), his last and most ambitious work with Clay, a three-act comic opera with full orchestra. He also found time to write two serious works, Broken Hearts (1875) and Dan'l Druce, Blacksmith (1876) and his most successful comic play, Engaged (1877), which inspired Oscar Wilde's The Importance of Being Earnest.

It was only by 1877 that Carte finally assembled enough investors to form the Comedy Opera Company with a mandate to launch a series of original English comic operas, beginning with a third collaboration between Gilbert and Sullivan, The Sorcerer, in November 1877.

The Sorcerer (1877), ran for 178 performances, a success by the standards of the day, but H.M.S. Pinafore (1878), which followed it, turned Gilbert and Sullivan into an international phenomenon. The bright and cheerful music of Pinafore was composed during a time when Sullivan was in the middle of a health scare. He was in terrible pain from a kidney stone. H.M.S. Pinafore ran for 571 performances in

London, the then-second-longest theatrical run in history, it also gave birth to and more than 150 unauthorised productions in America alone. Although this increased the reach of their reputations it added nothing to their profits.

It was noted in the Times review of H.M.S. Pinafore that the opera was an early attempt at the establishment of a "national musical stage" ... free from risqué French "improprieties" and without the "aid" of Italian and German musical models.

As the profits rolled in came acrimony among the investors who felt the shares were unequal. One night the other Comedy Opera Company partners hired thugs to storm the theatre to steal the sets and costumes in order that they could mount a rival production. This was beaten off by stagehands and others at the theatre loyal to Carte. Carte was to now continue as sole impresario of the newly renamed D'Oyly Carte Opera Company.

For the next decade, the Savoy Operas were Gilbert's principal activity. The successful comic operas with Sullivan continued to appear every year or two, several of them being among the longest-running productions of the musical stage. After Pinafore came The Pirates of Penzance (1879), Patience (1881), Iolanthe (1882), Princess Ida (1884 and based on Gilbert's earlier farce, The Princess), The Mikado (1885), Ruddigore (1887), The Yeomen of the Guard (1888), and The Gondoliers (1889). Gilbert not only directed and oversaw all aspects of production, but he designed the costumes himself for Patience, Iolanthe, Princess Ida, and Ruddigore. He insisted on precise and authentic sets and costumes, which provided a foundation to ground and focus his absurd characters and situations.

In 1878, Gilbert realised a lifelong dream to play Harlequin, which he did at the Gaiety Theatre in an amateur charity production of The Forty Thieves, written partly by himself. Gilbert trained for Harlequin's stylised dancing with his friend John D'Auban, who had arranged the dances for some of his plays and would choreograph most of the Gilbert and Sullivan operas. Producer John Hollingshead later remembered, "the gem of the performance was the grimly earnest and determined Harlequin of W. S. Gilbert. It gave me an idea of what Oliver Cromwell would have made of the character."

In 1879, Sullivan suggested to a reporter from The New York Times the secret of his success with Gilbert: "His ideas are as suggestive for music as they are quaint and laughable. His numbers ... always give me musical ideas."

During this time, Gilbert and Sullivan also collaborated on one other major work. In 1880, Sullivan was appointed director of the triennial Leeds Music Festival. For his first festival he was commissioned to write a sacred choral work. He chose Henry Hart Milman's 1822 dramatic poem based on the life and death of Saint Margaret the Virgin for its basis. It premiered at the Leeds music festival in October 1880. Gilbert arranged the original epic poem by Henry Hart Milman into a libretto suitable for the music.

Carte opened the next Gilbert and Sullivan piece, Patience, in April 1881 at London's Opera Comique, where their past three operas had played. In October, Patience transferred to the new, larger, state-of-the-art (it was the first theatre to be lit entirely with electricity) Savoy Theatre, built with the profits of the previous Gilbert and Sullivan works.

From now on all of the partnership's collaborations were produced at the Savoy. The first to actually premiere here was Iolanthe in 1882, it was their fourth hit in a row.

Cracks were beginning to surface between the partners. Sullivan, despite the financial security, began to view his work with Gilbert as beneath his skills, as well as being repetitious. After Iolanthe, Sullivan had not intended to write a new work with Gilbert, but when his broker went bankrupt in late 1882 he suffered serious financial loss. Needs must and Sullivan buckled down to continue writing Savoy operas. In February 1883, he and Gilbert signed a five-year agreement with Carte, requiring them to produce a new comic opera on six months' notice.

The ever watchful Gilbert had the previous year installed a telephone in his home and another at the prompt desk at the Savoy Theatre, so that he could listen in on performances and rehearsals from his home study. Gilbert had referred to the new technology in Pinafore in 1878, only two years after the device was invented and before London even had telephones.

Better news arrived for Sullivan on May 22nd, 1883, when he was knighted by Queen Victoria for his "services ... rendered to the promotion of the art of music" in Britain. The musical establishment, and many critics, believed that this would put an end to his career as a composer of comic opera – that a musical knight should not stoop below oratorio or grand opera. But Sullivan having just signed the five-year agreement and the financial security that gave him could no nothing to change course now.

The next opera, Princess Ida in 1884, which was the duo's only three-act, blank verse work, stuttered. Its run was much shorter. Sullivan's score was praised but with box office receipts lagging in March 1884, Carte gave the six months' notice, under the partnership contract, requiring a new opera.

Sullivan's friend, composer Frederic Clay, had suffered a serious stroke in early December 1883 that ended his career at only 45 years of age. Sullivan, with his own longstanding kidney problems, and his desire to devote himself to more serious music, replied to Carte, "It is impossible for me to do another piece of the character of those already written by Gilbert and myself."

Gilbert however was already at work on it. His idea revolved around a plot in which people fell in love against their wills after taking a magic lozenge. Sullivan was unequoviacal in his response. On April 1st, 1884 he wrote that he had "come to the end of my tether with the operas. I have been continually keeping down the music in order that not one syllable should be lost.... I should like to set a story of human interest & probability where the humorous words would come in a humorous not serious situation, & where, if the situation were a tender or dramatic one the words would be of similar character."

There was now a lengthy exchange of correspondence in which Sullivan called Gilbert's plot sketch (particularly the "lozenge" element) unacceptably mechanical, and too similar in both its grotesque "elements of topsyturveydom" and in actual plot to their earlier work, especially The Sorcerer, and requested, time and again, that a new subject be found.

This impasse was finally resolved on May 8th when Gilbert proposed a plot that would be their most successful: The Mikado (1885). It was to run for a staggering 672 performances.

In 1886, Sullivan composed his last large-scale choral work of the decade. It was a cantata for the Leeds Festival, The Golden Legend, based on Longfellow's poem of the same name. Apart from the comic operas, this proved to be Sullivan's best received full-length work. It was given hundreds of performances during his lifetime alone.

Ruddigore followed The Mikado in 1887. It was profitable, but its nine-month run was deemed to be disappointing compared with the earlier Savoy operas.

Gilbert was always keen to use a good idea again and proposed for their next piece another version of the magic lozenge plot. It was immediately rejected by Sullivan. Gilbert finally proposed a quite serious opera, to which Sullivan was in agreement. Although not a grand opera, The Yeomen of the Guard (1888) gave him the opportunity to compose his most ambitious stage work to date. In 1885, Sullivan had told an interviewer, ""The opera of the future is a compromise (among the French, German and Italian schools) – a sort of eclectic school, a selection of the merits of each one. I myself will make an attempt to produce a grand opera of this new school. ... Yes, it will be an historical work, and it is the dream of my life."

After The Yeomen of the Guard opened, Sullivan turned once again to Shakespeare and composed incidental music for Henry Irving's production of Macbeth (1888).

Sullivan wished to produce further serious works with Gilbert. He had collaborated with no other librettist since 1875. Gilbert felt the reaction to The Yeomen of the Guard had "not been so convincing as to warrant us in assuming that the public want something more earnest still." Gilbert countered by proposing that Sullivan should go ahead with his plan to write a grand opera, as well as comic works for the Savoy. Sullivan was not immediately persuaded. He replied, "I have lost the liking for writing comic opera, and entertain very grave doubts as to my power of doing it."

Nevertheless, Sullivan soon commissioned a grand opera libretto from Julian Sturgis (the recommendation came from Gilbert), while suggesting to Gilbert that he revive an old idea for an opera set in colourful Venice. The comic opera was completed first in 1889. The Gondoliers has been described as a pinnacle of Sullivan's achievement. It was to be the last great Gilbert and Sullivan success.

In April 1890, during the run of The Gondoliers, Gilbert objected to Carte's financial accounts which included a charge to the partnership for the cost of new carpeting for the Savoy Theatre lobby. Gilbert believed that this was a maintenance expense that should be charged to Carte alone. Carte who was building a new theatre to present Sullivan's forthcoming grand opera was adamant that it was legitimate. Sullivan sided with Carte, even going so far as to testify erroneously as to certain old debts.

The partners were in fundamental disagreement and the relationship was for all intents and purposes ruptured.

Gilbert took legal action against Carte and Sullivan and refused to write a word more for the Savoy. Sullivan wrote to Gilbert in September 1890 that he was "physically and mentally ill over this wretched business. I have not yet got over the shock of seeing our names coupled ... in hostile antagonism over a few miserable pounds".

From Gilbert's point of view Carte had either made a series of serious blunders in the accounts, or deliberately attempted to swindle his partners.

Gilbert wrote to Sullivan on May 28th, 1891, a year after the end of the "Quarrel", that Carte had admitted "an unintentional overcharge of nearly £1,000 in the electric lighting accounts alone." It seemed to illustrate Gilbert's point.

Work beckoned for Gilbert and he got on with it. He wrote The Mountebanks with Alfred Cellier and then a flop Haste to the Wedding with George Grossmith. Sullivan wrote Haddon Hall with Sydney Grundy.

In the Courts Gilbert prevailed in the lawsuit and felt vindicated. Although there was acrimony and bitterness between them the partnership had been so profitable that, after the financial failure of the Royal English Opera House, Carte and his wife sought to reunite the author and composer.

In 1891, after numerous failed attempts at a reconciliation, Tom Chappell, the music publisher who printed the Gilbert and Sullivan operas, stepped in to mediate between his two most profitable artists, and within two weeks, against the odds, had succeeded. The result was to be two more operas: Utopia, Limited (1893) and The Grand Duke (1896).

A third was almost achieved when Gilbert offered a third libretto to Sullivan (His Excellency, 1894), but his insistence on casting Nancy McIntosh, his protegée from Utopia, led to Sullivan's refusal.

Utopia, was only a modest success, and The Grand Duke, in which a theatrical troupe, by means of a "statutory duel" and a conspiracy, takes political control of a grand duchy, was a failure.

The partnership now ended for good.

Graciously Gilbert would late write, "... Savoy opera was snuffed out by the deplorable death of my distinguished collaborator, Sir Arthur Sullivan. When that event occurred, I saw no one with whom I felt that I could work with satisfaction and success, and so I discontinued to write libretti."

WS Gilbert – Life After the Partnership

In 1889 Gilbert financed the building of the Garrick Theatre. The following year the Gilberts moved to Grim's Dyke in Harrow. In 1891, Gilbert was appointed Justice of the Peace for Middlesex. After casting Nancy McIntosh in Utopia, Limited, he and Lady Gilbert developed an affection for her, and she eventually gained the status of an unofficially adopted daughter, moving to Grim's Dyke to live with them. She continued living there, even after Gilbert's death, until Lady Gilbert's death in 1936.

Although Gilbert announced a retirement from the theatre after the poor initial run of his last work with Sullivan, The Grand Duke (1896) and the poor reception of his 1897 play The Fortune Hunter, he produced at least three more plays over the last dozen years of his life, including an unsuccessful opera, Fallen Fairies (1909), with Edward German.

Gilbert, as we know was very keen on keeping his plays in the shape they were originally intended and continued to supervise the various revivals of his works by the D'Oyly Carte Opera Company, including its London Repertory seasons in 1906–09.

The last play he wrote, The Hooligan, produced just four months before his death, is a study of a young condemned thug in a prison cell. Gilbert shows sympathy for his protagonist, the son of a thief who, brought up among thieves, kills his girlfriend.

This grim, yet powerful piece, became one of Gilbert's most successful serious dramas, and it is easy to see why many thought he was developing a new style only for death to rob of us of what would surely be a fascinating journey.

In these last years, Gilbert wrote children's book versions of H.M.S. Pinafore and The Mikado giving, in some cases, backstory that is not found in the librettos.

Official recognition for him came on July 15th, 1907 with his knighthood in recognition of his contributions to drama. Gilbert was the first British writer ever to receive a knighthood for his plays alone—earlier dramatist knights were knighted for political and other services.

On May 29th, 1911, Gilbert was about to give a swimming lesson to Winifred Isabel Emery and 17-year-old Ruby Preece in the lake of his home, Grim's Dyke, when Preece lost her footing and called for help. Gilbert dived in to save her but suffered a heart attack in the middle of the lake and died.

William Schwenck was cremated at Golders Green and his ashes buried at the Church of St. John the Evangelist, Stanmore. The inscription on Gilbert's memorial on the south wall of the Thames Embankment in London reads: "His Foe was Folly, and his Weapon Wit".

George Grossmith wrote to The Daily Telegraph that, although Gilbert had been described as an autocrat at rehearsals, "That was really only his manner when he was playing the part of stage director at rehearsals. As a matter of fact, he was a generous, kind true gentleman, and I use the word in the purest and original sense."

Gilbert's legacy, aside from building the Garrick Theatre are the canon of Savoy Operas and other works that are either still being performed or in print all these years later. He has made a lasting and defining influence on both the American and British musical theatre. The innovations in content and form of the works that he and Sullivan developed, and in Gilbert's theories of acting and stage direction, directly influenced the development of the modern musical throughout the 20th century. Gilbert's lyrics use punning, as well as complex internal and two and three-syllable rhyme schemes, and served as a model for such 20th century Broadway lyricists as P.G. Wodehouse, Cole Porter, Ira Gershwin, and Lorenz Hart.

Gilbert's influence on the English language has also been marked, with well-known phrases such as "A policeman's lot is not a happy one", "short, sharp shock", "What never? Well, hardly ever!", and "let the punishment fit the crime" arising from his pen.

Arthur Sullivan – Life After the Partnership

Sullivan's only grand opera, Ivanhoe, based on Walter Scott's novel, opened at Carte's new Royal English Opera House on January 31st, 1891. Sullivan completed the score too late to meet Carte's planned production date, and costs had overrun to such an extent that Carte insisted on a contractual penalty of £3,000 for the delay. However, when it opened it ran 155 consecutive performances, a wonderful run for a serious opera, and garnered good reviews. Afterwards, Carte was unable to fill the new opera house with other productions, and, unfairly, Ivanhoe was blamed for the failure of the opera house.

Later in 1891, New York beckoned for Sullivan and his music for Tennyson's The Foresters, which ran at Daly's Theatre in New York in 1892, but failed in London the following year.

Sullivan returned to comic opera, but needed a new collaborator. His next piece was Haddon Hall in 1892, with a libretto by Sydney Grundy based somewhat loosely on the elopement of Dorothy Vernon with John Manners. Although still comic, the tone and style of the work was more serious and romantic than the operas with Gilbert. It nonetheless enjoyed a run of 204 performances, and earned critical praise.

In 1894 Sullivan teamed up again with F. C. Burnand for The Chieftain, a heavily-reworked version of their earlier two-act opera, The Contrabandista, alas it failed.

The following year Sullivan provided incidental music for the Lyceum, this time for J. Comyns Carr's King Arthur.

As we know Gilbert and Sullivan did reunite for The Grand Duke in 1896. But it failed and they never worked together again. This did not affect the constant revival of their earlier operas at the Savoy.

In May 1897, Sullivan's full-length ballet, Victoria and Merrie England, opened at the Alhambra Theatre in celebration of the Queen's Diamond Jubilee. The work's seven scenes celebrate English history and culture, with the Victorian period as the grand finale. It ran for six months which was a great achievement. Following this was The Beauty Stone in 1898, with a libretto by Arthur Wing Pinero and J. Comyns Carr. Based on mediaeval morality plays the opera was a critical failure and, on the whole, a commercial failure running for only seven weeks.

Success came in 1899, to benefit "the wives and children of soldiers and sailors" on active service in the Boer War, when Sullivan composed the music of a jingoistic song, "The Absent-Minded Beggar", to a text by Rudyard Kipling. It was a sensation and raised a staggering £250,000 from performances and the sale of sheet music and other merchandise. Later that year he returned to his comic roots with In The Rose of Persia, with a libretto by Basil Hood overlapping a setting of exotic Arabian Nights with plot elements of The Mikado. It was well received, and, apart from those with Gilbert, was his most successful full-length collaboration. Another opera with Hood, The Emerald Isle, quickly went into preparation, but sadly Sullivan died before it completion.

On November 22nd, 1900 Arthur Seymour Sullivan died of heart failure, following an attack of bronchitis, at his flat in London. The unfinished opera, The Emerald Isle, was completed by Edward German and premiered in 1901. His Te Deum Laudamus, written to commemorate the end of the Boer War, was performed posthumously.

Sullivan wished to be buried in Brompton Cemetery with his parents and brother, but by order of the Queen he was buried in St. Paul's Cathedral. In addition to his knighthood, honours awarded to Sullivan in his lifetime included Doctor in Music, honoris causa, by the universities of Cambridge (1876) and Oxford (1879); Chevalier, Légion d'honneur, France (1878); The Order of the Medjidieh conferred by the Sultan of Turkey (1888); and appointment as a Member of the Fourth Class of the Royal Victorian Order (MVO) in 1897.

In all, Sullivan's artistic output included 23 operas, 13 major orchestral works, eight choral works and oratorios, two ballets, one song cycle, incidental music to several plays, numerous hymns and other church pieces, and a large body of songs, parlour ballads, part songs, carols, and piano and chamber pieces.

Although Sullivan had several long term affairs and was also known to have a roving eye that led him to frequent liaisons with many other women he never married.

Rachel Scott Russell was the first of his great loves. Her parents' disapproval meant they met secretly but by 1868, Sullivan was enmeshed in a simultaneous and secret affair with Rachel's sister Louise. Both relationships had ceased by early 1869.

Sullivan's affair with the American socialite, Fanny Ronalds, a woman three years his senior, who had two children began when they met in Paris around 1867. The affair began in earnest soon after she moved to London in 1871. Despite his wandering ways she was a constant companion up to the time of Sullivan's death, but around 1889 or 1890, the sexual relationship seems to have ended.

In 1896, the 54-year-old Sullivan proposed marriage to 22-year-old Violet Beddington but she refused.

The favourite playgrounds for Sullivan were Paris and the south of France, with friends ranging from European royalty to Claude Debussy, and where the casinos enabled him to indulge his passion for gambling.

Sullivan enjoyed playing tennis although, according to George Grossmith, "I have seen some bad lawn-tennis players in my time, but I never saw anyone so bad as Arthur Sullivan".

He was devoted to his parents, particularly his mother, until her death in 1882. Henry Lytton wrote, "I believe there was never a more affectionate tie than that which existed between Sullivan and his mother, a very witty old lady, and one who took an exceptional pride in her son's accomplishments.

Sullivan once explained his method of working; "I don't use the piano in composition – that would limit me terribly". Sullivan explained that he did not wait for inspiration, but had "to dig for it. ... I decide on the rhythm before I come to the question of melody. ... I mark out the metre in dots and dashes, and not until I have quite settled on the rhythm do I proceed to actual notation."

In composing the Savoy operas, Sullivan wrote the vocal lines of the musical numbers first, and these were given to the actors. He, or an assistant, improvised a piano accompaniment at the early rehearsals; he wrote the orchestrations later, after he had seen what Gilbert's stage business would be. He left the overtures until last and often delegated their composition, based on his outlines, to his assistants, often adding his suggestions or corrections. Those Sullivan wrote himself include Thespis, Iolanthe, Princess Ida, The Yeomen of the Guard, The Gondoliers, The Grand Duke and probably Utopia Limited. Most of the overtures are structured as a potpourri of tunes from the operas in three sections: fast, slow and fast. The overtures from the Gilbert and Sullivan operas remain popular. Sullivan invariably conducted the operas on their opening nights.

In general, Sullivan preferred to write in major keys. In the Savoy operas less than 5% of the numbers are in a minor key and even in his serious works the major prevails. Sullivan was happy on occasion to use chords traditionally considered technically incorrect. When reproached for using consecutive fifths in Cox and Box, he replied "if 5ths turn up it doesn't matter, so long as there is no offence to the ear."

Sullivan's orchestra for the Savoy Operas was typical of any other pit orchestra of his era: 2 flutes (+ piccolo), oboe, 2 clarinets, bassoon, 2 horns, 2 cornets, 2 trombones, timpani, percussion and strings. According to Geoffrey Toye, the number of players in the Savoy orchestra was originally 31. Sullivan argued hard for an increase in the pit orchestra's size, and starting with The Yeomen of the Guard, the orchestra was augmented with a second bassoon and a bass trombone. Sullivan generally orchestrated each score at almost the last moment, noting that the accompaniment for an opera had to wait until he saw the staging, so that he could judge how heavily or lightly to orchestrate each part of the music. For his large-scale orchestral pieces, Sullivan added a second oboe part, sometimes double bassoon and bass clarinet, more horns, trumpets, tuba, and sometimes an organ and/or a harp. Many of these pieces used very large orchestras.

Sullivan's critical reputation has undergone extreme changes since he first came to prominence in the 1860s. At first, critics were struck by his potential, and he was hailed as the long-awaited great English composer. His incidental music to The Tempest received an acclaimed premiere at the Crystal Palace just before Sullivan's 20th birthday in April 1862. The Athenaeum wrote:

When Sullivan turned to comic opera with Gilbert, the serious critics began to express disapproval. Peter Gammond writes of "misapprehensions and prejudices, delivered to our door by the Victorian firm Musical Snobs Ltd. ... frivolity and high spirits were sincerely seen as elements that could not be exhibited by anyone who was to be admitted to the sanctified society of Art." As early as 1877 The Figaro wrote that Sullivan "has all the ability to make him a great composer, but he wilfully throws his opportunity away. ... He possesses all the natural ability to have given us an English opera, and, instead, he affords us a little more-or-less excellent fooling." Few critics denied the excellence of Sullivan's theatre scores. The Theatre wrote that "Iolanthe sustains Dr Sullivan's reputation as the most spontaneous, fertile, and scholarly composer of comic opera this country has ever produced." However, comic opera, no matter how skilfully crafted, was viewed as an intrinsically lower form of art than oratorio. The Athenaeum's review of The Martyr of Antioch declared: "It is an advantage to have the composer of H.M.S. Pinafore occupying himself with a worthier form of art."

Although the more solemn members of the musical establishment could not forgive Sullivan for writing music that was both comic and accessible, he was, nevertheless, "the nation's de facto composer laureate".

Gilbert & Sullivan – A Concise Bibliography

The Collaborative Pieces

All of these operas are full-length two-act works, except for Trial by Jury, which is in one act, and Princess Ida, which is three acts.

Thespis (1871)
Trial by Jury (1875)
The Sorcerer (1877)
H.M.S. Pinafore (1878)
The Pirates of Penzance (1879)
Patience (1881)

Iolanthe (1882)
Princess Ida (1884)
The Mikado (1885)
Ruddigore (1887)
The Yeomen of the Guard (1888)
The Gondoliers (1889)
Utopia, Limited (1893)
The Grand Duke (1896)

W.S. Gilbert – his Other Works

Poetry

The Bab Ballads, a collection of comic verse published roughly between 1865 and 1871
Songs of a Savoyard, London, 1890, a collection of Gilbert's song lyrics.

Short Stories

Foggerty's Fairy & Other Tales, a collection of short stories and essays, mainly from before 1874.

Some other short stories but not in the above appear here:-

Belgravia, Vol. 2 (1867). "From St. Paul's to Piccadilly," pp. 67–74
Fun, Vol. 1 new series (1865-1866) (several contributions by Gilbert; near end of volume)
Fun Christmas Number 1865, ("The Astounding Adventure of Wheeler J. Calamity,")
London Society, Vol. 13 (1868) (three "Thumbnail Sketches" by Gilbert)
On the Cards: Routledge's Christmas Annual (1867) ("Diamonds," and "The Converted Clown,")

Other Books

The Pinafore Picture Book, 1908, retelling the story of H.M.S. Pinafore for children, in prose narrative
The Story of The Mikado, 1921, a similar retelling of The Mikado for children

Plays and Musical Stage Works
Selected stage works that were important to Gilbert's career or were otherwise notable, in chronological order, excluding those listed under other headings below:

Dulcamara, or the Little Duck and the Great Quack (1866)
La Vivandière (1867)
Harlequin Cock Robin and Jenny Wren (1867), a Christmas pantomime.
The Merry Zingara (1868)
Robert the Devil (1868), it opened the Gaiety Theatre, London and ran in the provinces for 3 years.
The Pretty Druidess (1869), a parody of Norma – the last of Gilbert's five "operatic burlesques"
An Old Score (1869) (rewritten as "Quits!" in 1872) Gilbert's first full-length comedy.
The Princess (1870). Musical farce; the precursor to Princess Ida.
The Palace of Truth (1870).

Creatures of Impulse (1871), music by Alberto Randegger. From Gilberts story "A Strange Old Lady".
Pygmalion and Galatea (1871).
Randall's Thumb (1871). A comedy that opened the Royal Court Theatre.
The Wicked World (1873).
The Happy Land (1873). This work was briefly banned for its sharp satire of government ministers.
The Realm of Joy (1873).
The Wedding March (1873) a farce adapted from Un Chapeau de Paille d'Italie.
Rosencrantz & Guildenstern (published 1874, performed 1891). Gilbert's burlesque of Hamlet.
Charity (1874). Concerns Victorian attitudes towards sex outside of marriage.
Sweethearts (1874).
Tom Cobb (1875).
Broken Hearts (1875). The last of Gilbert's "fairy comedies", this was one of Gilbert's favourite plays.
Dan'l Druce, Blacksmith (1876).
Engaged (1877).
The Ne'er-do-Weel (1878); rewritten as "The Vagabond" after a few weeks.
The Forty Thieves (1878). Co-written with three other writers, WSG played Harlequin.
Gretchen (1879)
Foggerty's Fairy (1881)
Brantinghame Hall (1888) Gilbert's biggest flop, it sent producer Rutland Barrington into bankruptcy.
The Fortune Hunter (1897). Its reception provoked WSG to announce retiring from writing for the stage.
The Fairy's Dilemma (1904).
The Hooligan (1911).

German Reed Entertainments
Gilbert wrote six one-act musical entertainments for the German Reeds between 1869 and 1875. They were successful in their own right and also helped form Gilbert's mature style as a dramatist.

No Cards (1869)
Ages Ago (1869). Gilbert's first collaboration with Frederic Clay, ran for 350 performances.
Our Island Home (1870)
A Sensation Novel (1871)
Happy Arcadia (1872)
Eyes and No Eyes (1875)

Early Comic Operas
The Gentleman in Black (1870; music by Frederic Clay). The score is lost.
Les Brigands (1871), an English adaptation of Jacques Offenbach's operetta.
Topsyturveydom (1874; music by Alfred Cellier). The score is lost.
Princess Toto (1876; music by Frederic Clay). A three-act opera.

Later Operas (Without Sullivan)
Though not as popular as the works with Arthur Sullivan, a few of Gilbert's later works arguably have stronger plots than the last two Gilbert and Sullivan operas.

The Mountebanks (1892; music; Alfred Cellier). This is the "lozenge plot" that Sullivan declined to set on several occasions.

Haste to the Wedding (1892; music; George Grossmith). An unsuccessful adaptation of The Wedding March.

His Excellency (1894; music; Osmond Carr). Gilbert felt that if Sullivan had set it, the piece would have been "another Mikado".

Fallen Fairies (1909; music by Edward German). Gilbert's last opera, which was a failure.

Parlour Ballads

The Yarn of the Nancy Bell, with music by Alfred Plumpton. One of the Bab Ballads. 1869.

Thady O'Flynn, with music by James L. Molloy. 1868. From No Cards.

Would You Know that Maiden Fair, with music by Frederic Clay. From Ages Ago. c. 1869.

Corisande, with music by James L. Molloy. 1870.

Eily's Reason, with music by James L. Molloy. 1871.

Three songs from A Sensation Novel: "The Detective's Song", "The Tyrannical Bridegroom", and "The Jewel". 1871

The Distant Shore, with music by Arthur Sullivan. 1874.

The Love that Loves me Not, with music by Arthur Sullivan. 1875.

Sweethearts, with music by Arthur Sullivan. 1875.

Let Me Stay, with music by Walter Maynard. 1875.

Arthur Sullivan – His Other Works

Operas

The Sapphire Necklace (ca. 1863; unperformed)

Cox and Box (1866)

The Contrabandista (1867)

The Zoo (1875)

Ivanhoe (1891)

Haddon Hall (1892)

The Chieftain (1894)

The Beauty Stone (1898)

The Rose of Persia (1899)

The Emerald Isle (1901; completed by Edward German)

Incidental Music to Plays

The Tempest (1861)

The Merchant of Venice (1871)

The Merry Wives of Windsor (1874)

Henry VIII (1877)

Macbeth (1888)

Tennyson's The Foresters (1892)

J. Comyns Carr's King Arthur for Henry Irving (1895)

Ballets and Song Cycle
L'Île Enchantée (1864 ballet)
Victoria and Merrie England (1897 ballet)
The Window; or, The Song of the Wrens (1871 song cycle)

Choral Works with Orchestra
The Masque at Kenilworth (1864)
The Prodigal Son (Sullivan) (1869)
On Shore and Sea (1871)
Festival Te Deum (1872)
The Light of the World (Sullivan) (1873)
The Martyr of Antioch (1880)
Ode for the Opening of the Colonial and Indian Exhibition (1886)
The Golden Legend (1886)
Ode for the Laying of the Foundation Stone of The Imperial Institute (1887)
Te Deum Laudamus (1902; performed posthumously)

Orchestral Works
Overture in D (1858; now lost)
Overture The Feast of Roses (1860; now lost)
Procession March (1863)
Princess of Wales's March (1863)
Symphony in E, "Irish" (1866)
Overture in C, "In Memoriam" (1866)
Concerto for Cello and Orchestra (1866)
Overture Marmion (1867)
Overture di Ballo (1870)
Imperial March (1893)
The Absent-Minded Beggar March (1899)

Other Works

Songs & Parlour Ballads
Absent-minded Beggar (Rudyard Kipling) 1899
Arabian Love Song (Percy Bysshe Shelley) 1866
Ay de mi, My Bird (George Eliot)1874
Bid me at least Goodbye (Sydney Grundy) 1894
Birds in the Night (Lionel H. Lewin) 1869
Bride from the North (Henry F. Chorley) 1863
Care is all Fiddle-dee-dee (F. C. Burnand) 1874
Chorister, The (Fred. E. Weatherly) 1876
Christmas Bells at Sea (C. L. Kenney) 1875

County Guy (Walter Scott) 1867
Distant Shore, The (W. S. Gilbert) 1874
Dove Song (William Brough) 1869
E tu nol sai - see You Sleep (G. Mazzucato) 1889
Edward Gray (Alfred Tennyson)(1880
Ever (Mrs Bloomfield Moore) 1887
First Departure - see The Chorister (Rev. E. Munroe) 1874
Give (Adelaide Anne Procter) 1867
Golden Days (Lionel H. Lewin)1872
Guinevere! (Lionel H. Lewin) 1872
I Heard the Nightingale (Rev. C. H. Townsend) 1863
I Wish to Tune my Quiv'ring Lyre (Anacreon; trans. Lord Byron) 1868
I Would I were a King (Victor Hugo; trans. A. Cockburn) 1878
Ich möchte hinaus es jauchzen (A. Corrodi) 1859
If Doughty Deeds (Robert Graham of Gartmore) 1866
In the Summers Long Ago (J. P. Douglas) 1867
Let Me Dream Again (B. C. Stephenson) 1875
Lied, mit Thränen halbgeschrieben (Eichendorff)1861
Life that Lives for You (Lionel H. Lewin) 1870
Little Darling Sleep Again (Cradle Song) (anon) 1874
Living Poems (H. W. Longfellow)1874
Longing for Home (Jean Ingelow) 1904
Looking Back (Louisa Gray)1870
Looking Forward (Louisa Gray) 1873
Lost Chord, The (Adelaide Anne Procter) 1877
Love that Loves Me Not, The (W. S. Gilbert) 1875
Maiden's Story, The (Emma Embury) 1867
Marquis de Mincepie, The (F. C. Burnand) 1874
Mary Morison (Robert Burns) 1874
Moon in Silent Brightness, The (Bishop Reginald Heber) 1868
Mother's Dream, The (Rev. W. Barnes) 1868
My Dear and Only Love (Marquis of Montrose) 1874
My Dearest Heart (anon) 1874
My Heart is like a Silent Lute (Benjamin Disraeli) 1904
My Love - see "There Sits a Bird in Yonder Tree
My Love Beyond the Sea - see "In the Summers Long Ago"
None but I Can Say (Lionel H. Lewin)1872
O Fair Dove, O Fond Dove (Jean Ingelow) 1868
O Israel (Hosea) 1855
O Mistress Mine (William Shakespeare) 1866
O Swallow, Swallow (Alfred Tennyson) 1900
Oh Sweet and Fair (A. F. C. K.) 1868
Oh! bella mia - see "Oh! Ma Charmante"
Oh! Ma Charmante (Victor Hugo) 1872
Old Love Letters (S. K. Cowen) 1879
Once Again (Lionel H. Lewin) 1872
Orpheus with his Lute (William Shakespeare) 1866
River, The (anon) 1875

Roads Should Blossom, The (anon) 1864
Rosalind (William Shakespeare) 1866
Sad Memories (C. J. Rowe) 1869
Sailor's Grave, The (H. F. Lyte) 1872
St. Agnes' Eve (Alfred Tennyson) 1879
Shadow, A. (Adelaide Anne Procter)1886
She is not Fair to Outward View (Hartley Coleridge) 1866
Sigh no More, Ladies (William Shakespeare) 1866
Sleep My Love, Sleep (R. Whyte Melville) 1874
Snow Lies White, The (Jean Ingelow) 1868
Sometimes (Lady Lindsay of Balcarres) 1877
Sweet Day So Cool (George Herbert) 1864
Sweet Dreamer - see "Oh! Ma Charmante"
Sweethearts (W. S. Gilbert) 1875
Tears, Idle Tears (Alfred Tennyson) 1900
Tender and True (Dinah Maria Mulock) 1874
There Sits a Bird on Yonder TreeRev. (C. H. Barham) 1873
Thou art Lost to Me (anon) 1865
Thou art Weary (Adelaide Anne Procter) 1874
Thou'rt Passing Hence (Felicia Hemans) 1875
To One in Paradise (Edgar Allan Poe) 1904
Troubadour, The (Walter Scott) 1869
Village Chimes, The (C. J. Rowe) 1870
Weary Lot is Thine, Fair Maid, A (Walter Scott) 1866
We've Ploughed our Land (anon)1875
When Thou Art Near (W. J. Stewart) 1877
White Plume, The - see "The Bride from the North"
Will He Come? (Adelaide A. Procter) 1865
Willow Song, The (William Shakespeare)1866
You Sleep (B. C. Stephenson) 1889

Hymns (Title & First Line)
Adoro Te - Saviour, again to Thy dear name we raise (Arranger)
All This Night - All this night bright angels sing
Angel Voices - Angel voices, ever singing
Audite Audientes me - I heard the voice of Jesus say
Bethlehem - While shepherd's watched their flocks (Arranger)
Bishopgarth - O King of Kings, Whose reign of old
Bolwell - Thou to whom the sick and dying
Carrow - My God, I thank Thee Who has made
Chapel Royal - O love that wilt not let me go
Christus - Show me not only Jesus dying
Clarence - Winter reigneth o'er the land
Coena Domini - Draw nigh, and take the body of the Lord
Come Unto Me - Come unto Me, ye weary (Arranger)
Constance - I've found a Friend; oh, such a Friend
Coronae - Crown Him, with many crowns

Courage, Brother - Courage, brother, do not stumble
Dominion Hymn - God bless our wide dominion
Dulce Sonans - Angel voices, ever singing
Ecclesia - The church has waited long
Ellers - Saviour, again to Thy dear name we raise (Arranger)
Evelyn - In the hour of my distress
Ever Faithful - Let us with a gladsome mind
Fatherland (St. Edmund) - I'm but a stranger here
Formosa (Falfield) - Love Divine, all love excelling
Fortunatus - Welcome, happy morning!
Golden Sheaves - To Thee, O Lord, our hearts we raise
Hanford - Jesu, my Saviour, look on me
Heber (Gennesareth) - When through the torn sail
Holy City - Sing Alleluia forth in duteous praise
Hushed was the Evening Hymn - Hushed was the evening hymn
Hymn of the Homeland - The homeland, the homeland
Lacrymae - Lord, in this Thy mercy's day
Leominster - A few more years shall roll (Arranger)
Light - Holy Spirit! Come in might! (Arranger)
Litany (1) - Jesu, life of those who die
Litany (2) - Jesu, we are far away
Long Home, The - Tender Shepherd, Thou hast still'd
Lux eoi - All is bright and cheeful round us
Lux in Tenebris - Lead, kindly Light
Lux Mundi - O Jesu, Thou art standing
Marlborough - O Strength and Stay, upholding all creation (Arranger)
Mount Zion - Rock of Ages, cleft for me
Nearer Home - For ever with the Lord (Arranger)
Noel - It came upon the midnight clear (Arranger)
Old 137th - Great King of nations, hear our prayer (Arranger)
Paradise - O Paradise!
Parting - With the sweet word of peace (Arranger)
Pilgrimage - From Egypt's bondage come
Promissio Patris - Our blest Redeemer, ere He breathed
Propior Deo - Nearer, my God, to Thee
Rest - Art thou weary, art thou languid
Resurrexit - Christ is risen!
Roseate Hues, The - The roseate hues of early dawn
Safe Home - Safe home, safe home in port
St. Ann - The Son of God goes forth to war (Arranger)
St. Francis - O Father, who hast created all
St. Gertrude - Onward, Christian soldiers
St. Kevin - Come, ye faithful, raise the strain
St. Lucian - Of Thy love some gracious token
St. Luke (St. Nathaniel) - God moves in a mysterious way
St. Mary Magdalene - Saviour, when in dust to Thee
St. Millicent - Let no tears to-day be shed
St. Patrick - He is gone - a cloud of light

St. Theresa - Brightly gleams our banner
Saints of God - The Saints of God, their conflict past.
Springtime - For all Thy love and goodness (Arranger)
Strain Upraise, The - The Strain upraise in joy and praise
Thou God of Love - Thou God of Love, beneath Thy sheltering wing
Ultor Omnipotens - God the all terrible! King who ordainest
Valete - Sweet Saviour, bless us 'ere we go
Veni, Creator - Come Holy Ghost, our souls inspire
Victoria - To mourn our dead we gather here

Part Songs

The term "Part Song" is more usually applied to one where the highest part carries the melody with the other voices supplying the accompanying harmonies.

Also included here are the soprano duet, The Sisters, and the trio Sullivan composed for the play Olivia by W. G. Wills, Morn, Happy Morn.

O Lady Dear (Madrigal) - Composed 1857, unpublished.
It was a Lover and his Lass - Words by Shakespeare. Performed at the Royal Academy of Music, 1857, unpublished.
Seaside Thoughts - Words by Bernard Bartram. Composed 1857. Published 1904.
The Last Night of the Year - Words by H. F. Chorley. Published 1863.
O Hush Thee, My Babie - Words by Walter Scott. Published 1867.
The Rainy Day - Words by H. W. Longfellow. Published 1867.
Evening - Words by Lord Houghton, after Goethe. Published 1868.
Parting Gleams - Words by Aubrey de Vere. Published 1868.
Echoes - Words by Thomas Moore. Published 1868.
The Long Day Closes - Words by H. F. Chorley. Published 1868.
Joy to the Victors - Words by Walter Scott. Published 1868
The Beleaguered - Words by H. F. Chorley. Published 1868.
It Came Upon the Midnight Clear - Words by E. H. Sears. Published 1871.
Lead, Kindly Light - Words by J. H. Newman. Published 1871.
Through Sorrows Path - Words by H. Kirke White. Published 1871.
Say, Watchman, What of the Night? - Words from Isaiah. Published 1871.
The Way is Long and Dreary - Words by Adelaide Anne Procter. Published 1871.
Morn, Happy Morn - Composed for the play, Olivia by W. G. Wills. Published 1878.
The Sisters - Words by Alfred Tennyson. Published 1881.
Wreaths for our Graves - Words by L. F. Massey. Published 1898.
Fair Daffodils - Words by Robert Herrick. Published 1904.

Church Songs

By the Waters of Babylon - Composed c. 1850. Unpublished.
Sing unto the Lord - Composed 1855. Unpublished.
Psalm 103 - Composed 1856. Unpublished.
We have heard with our ears

(i) Dedicated to Sir George Smart and performed at the Chapel Royal, January 1860.

(ii) Dedicated to Rev. Thomas Helmore. 1865.

O Love the Lord - Dedicated to John Goss. 1864.

Te Deum, Jubilate, Kyrie (in D major) 1866.

O God, Thou art Worthy - Composed for the wedding of Adrian Hope, 3 June 1867. Published in 1871.

O Taste and See - Dedicated to Rev. C. H. Haweis. 1867.

Rejoice in the Lord - Composed for the wedding of Rev. R. Brown-Borthwick, 16 April 1868.

Sing, O Heavens - Dedicated to Rev. F. C. Byng. 1869.

I Will Worship - Dedicated to Rev. F. Gore Ouseley. 1871.

Two Choruses adapted from Russian Church Music, 1874.

(i) Turn Thee Again

(ii) Mercy and Truth

I Will Mention Thy Loving-kindness - Dedicated to John Stainer. 1875.

I Will Sing of Thy Power. 1877.

Hearken Unto Me, My People. 1877.

Turn Thy Face. 1878.

Who is Like unto Thee - Dedicated to Walter Parratt. 1883.

I Will Lay Me Down in Peace - Composed 1868. Published only in 1910.

Christmas Carols & Songs

Advent

Hearken unto me, my people - An Anthem for Advent or General Use. Words from Isaiah. (1877)

Christmas Carols

All this night bright angels sing - Words by W. Austin. (1870)

I Sing the Birth - Words by Ben Jonson. (1868)

It Came Upon the Midnight Clear - Words by E. H. Sears.

Part Song for Soprano Solo and Choir (1871)

Hymn Tune "Noel" (1874)

Upon the Snow-clad Earth (1876)

While Shepherds Watched - Words by Nahum Tate (1874)

Hark! What Mean those Holy Voices? - Words by John Cawood (1883)

Songs

Christmas Bells at Sea - Words by Charles Kenney (1875)

Two songs from The Miller and His Man - A Christmas Drawing Room Entertainment. Words by F. C. Burnand (1874)

The Marquis de Mincepie

Care is all Fiddle-dee-dee

The Last Night of the Year - Part Song - Words by H. F. Chorley (1863)

Chamber Music & Solo Piano

Scherzo - Piano Solo, 1857, unpublished.

Capriccio No. 2 - Piano Solo (unfinished), 1857, unpublished.
String Quartet - Performed at Leipzig, May 1859. Published 2000
Romance in G minor - For string quartet, 1859. Published 1964.
Thoughts - Two pieces for piano solo, Published by Cramer, 1862.
An Idyll - For Cello and Piano. Composed in 1865 and Published 1899.
Allegro Risoluto - Piano solo, 1866. Published only in 1974
Berceuse - Based on the theme of Hushed was the Bacon from Cox and Box but with additional material.
Day Dreams - Six pieces for piano solo. 1867
Duo Concertante - Cello and piano. 1868
Twilight - Piano solo. 1868

www.ingramcontent.com/pod-product-compliance
Lightning Source LLC
Chambersburg PA
CBHW060049050426
42448CB00011B/2369